BECOME A SPEEDDEMON:
PRODUCTIVITY TRICKS TO HAVE MORE TIME

By

JONATHAN LEVI

www.BecomeaSpeedDemon.com

J. LEVI PUBLISHING

J. Levi Publishing
SpeedDemon@jle.vi

Become a SpeedDemon: Productivity Tricks To Have More Time

ISBN-13: 978-0692503768
ISBN-10: 0692503765

To my students and fans in 186 countries and counting. You inspire me, energize me, and give my life added purpose.

From the bottom of my heart: Thank you.

FOREWORD

Hi,

My name is Ari Meisel, and for those of you who've never heard of me, I'm a husband, father, author, speaker, coach, and a HUGE fan of SpeedDemon.

To tell you why I love SpeedDemon, I need to tell you a little bit of my story...

Back in 2006, my life wasn't just good it was great. I was dating beautiful woman (now my wife), running a booming business, and making rock-solid money—for a young guy in his 20s, it was pretty much the dream.

Everything was humming along smoothly until one day I was absolutely gut-checked (both emotionally and physically) by a phone call from my doctor:

Crohn's Disease an incurable and utterly miserable autoimmune disorder.

Crohn's? How could I have Crohn's? Surely a mistake had been made.

But within a few weeks of that unexpected phone call, it because readily apparent that no error had been made—I began losing *massive* amounts of weight, my energy evaporated, and my physical strength plummeted. I had no appetite, no motivation, and no will to do anything except wallow in self-pity.

I remember thinking—*how could this happen to me? Why do I deserve to have my life derailed by sickness?*

The pity party continued for several months until one day I woke up and said, "To hell with this." I decided that if I wanted to actually LIVE my life, as opposed to just survive it, I would need to strap on my helmet and go to war with Crohn's.

Against the advice of doctors and loved-ones, I embarked upon an extremely painful journey to rid myself of this "incurable" disease—I began seeking ways to streamline my life, reduce stress, and improve my efficiency so I could invest as much of my limited energy as possible into getting healthy.

The journey was raw, excruciating, and real, laden with massive trials and massive errors. But no matter the pain, no matter the setbacks, I was conscious committed to doing *everything* in my power to strengthen an ever-weakening body.

It took more than 36 months of struggle, but one day in 2009, doctors told me they could find no signs or symptoms of Crohn's *anywhere* in my body.

It was a monumental personal victory, but one I wish I didn't have to achieve on my own.

If I didn't have to learn everything on my own through trial and error, my battle against Crohn's could have been so much easier.

And that's why I'm telling you this story...

If SpeedDemon had existed during the throes of my battle with Crohn's, I could have spent FAR less time mired in the trenches of experimentation, and more time driving the disease into surrender.

SpeedDemon is the perfect guide for anyone looking to discover the power of productivity, and escape the chaos of our increasingly high-speed world.

Jonathan spent *hundreds of hours* highlighting all the tips, tricks, and tools, you could ever need to live a healthier, happier life.

His steps and instructions are not only vivid and clear, but forged in his own life-experience. And his observations on the Pareto Principle, the power of "no," and the importance of "flow" aren't just accurate—they're bulls-eyes.

Whether you're battling a disease, or suffering from the stress of modern life, SpeedDemon is going to give you exactly what you need to start living life again.

Ari Meisel
http://lessdoing.com/

PREFACE

HOW TO USE THIS BOOK

For Further Research: At the end of some chapters, you will find a section called "For Further Research." Links for supplemental materials will be found in this section (articles, videos, apps, podcasts, etc.). The materials are an important part of the learning process. As an expert in accelerated learning, I can tell you that the best, most engaged students are those who take ownership in their learning experience and invest in independent learning. Be a proactive student and you will get much more out of the time you invest in reading this book!

THE BOOK AND THE COURSE

This book is a product of a bestselling Udemy course, which later grew into an in-depth MasterClass (**http://becomeaspeeddemon.com**). The MasterClass is a "live" creation, which continually grows and improves with the suggestions of students, and with the addition of various expert interviews. However, there are always students who prefer the feel of a book in their hands.

While comprehensive in its teachings, the book cannot (due to publication) be a "live" and growing product, and of course, some topics which are only suited to hands-on video demonstrations or interactive exercises have been removed. To keep up to date on the "latest and greatest," please consider joining the MasterClass.

TABLE OF CONTENTS

Section 1: Introductions & Foundations

CHAPTER 1: HOW THIS COURSE CAME TO BE

My name is Jonathan Levi. I am an entrepreneur, angel investor, life hacker, SuperLearner, and best-selling author of some of the most popular courses on the web today. In other words, I wear a lot of hats.

GETTING THE MOST OUT OF LIFE

For as long as I can remember, I have tried to get the most out of my life, my time, and my effort. While some may view this as cutting corners, in fact, I have always tried to eliminate waste and unnecessary effort in my life. Early on in my life, my mother and father taught me that it was better to work smart than to work hard – an ideal I do not think many parents openly teach their kids.

THE EARLY YEARS

My main interest and focus on "life hacking" or productivity came during my late teenage years. At age 16, I founded an e-commerce company selling luxury goods. That business grew much faster than I could have ever imagined, and by the time I started University at UC Berkeley, I was running a $2M business, all in my spare time. Since I wanted to maintain an "A" average, be an active member of my fraternity, have a healthy relationship with my girlfriend, and still have time to relax, I had to learn time management and productivity hacks – fast.

During this time, I was heavily influenced by a lot of different people. The greatest influencers were my parents, university professors, mentors, and, of course, the works of Tim Ferriss, a legendary productivity hacker, and, in my opinion, a total genius!

The productivity hacks I learned enabled me to grow my business 2X year-over-year during my entire 4-year career at Berkeley while maintaining a 3.9 average, a great social life, and tons of hobbies. Later on, these same techniques would help me serve as president of a nonprofit while at the same time running my company — in addition to two other side businesses.

WHERE I AM NOW

Fast forward a few years, and I found myself in a venture capital office. After selling my company, I was preparing to start a very intensive one-year, condensed business school program. I wanted to make sure I had time to learn all the material, as well as network, party, and travel throughout Europe and Southeast Asia. I needed even *more* strategies for maximizing my time and effort. As luck would have it (or perhaps kismet), it was at this time that I met an expert in speed-reading and mnemonics - or memory techniques.

I tell that story in my bestselling course, "*Become a SuperLearner,*" so I will not go into much detail here. However, it is important to note I left for business school with the incredible ability to read 800 words per minute with up to 80 or 90% retention. While this obviously helped me manage the academic load in record time, it also gave me a great new ability: I could synthesize and digest huge amounts of information *really* quickly.

In fact, everything I learned about creating and marketing a bestselling online course, I learned in approximately one afternoon of speed-reading. This enabled my course to skyrocket to the top of Udemy's

staff picks and bestsellers' lists in record time –
something other instructors spend weeks or months
figuring out, if at all.

In short, knowledge is definitely power, and in my
opinion, the ability to learn effectively is the "meta"
skill or "force multiplier" that enables you to
accomplish just about anything you set your mind to.

I believe in this to such an extent that I've
dedicated my life to it. At least for now.

LIFE HACKING

Since I have always been interested in "life
hacking," some of the first subjects I dove into (after
the stress of business school was behind me) were bio
hacks. I read a 660-page anthology of body language to
learn how to "hack" the elusive concept of charisma,
enabling me to stand in front of a camera and lecture
without being completely awkward. I read Kelly
Starrett's bookshelf-breaking book "*Becoming a
Supple Leopard*," on hacking and fixing your body to
alleviate chronic pain. Of course, I read Tim Ferriss'
awesome bio-hacking book, *The 4-Hour Body*.

I also devoured literally thousands of articles on
everything from sleep, computer productivity, cutting-
edge technology hacks, and more. I have done all kinds
of crazy tests and experiments on myself, and I love to
share the benefits of my learnings with others.

Today, I lead a very efficient life. I do not work or
stress too much. I hardly waste any time on menial
tasks. I run a few side businesses, work on a lot of
different projects, learn languages in my spare time,
and travel about 1 out of every 6 weeks. In short, I have
the capacity to make a lot of free time for things I
believe are worthwhile. In fact, having free time has
become so apparent to people who meet me, a lot of my
conversations inevitably become lectures on how to

shave time off the unimportant activities in life to make more time.

Therefore, the ability save time is what brings me to creating this course. Just as with "*Become a SuperLearner*," sharing all my different little hacks one by one with people over lunch has become extremely time consuming. Therefore, I decided to commit all those hacks to video – because after all, saving time is about not only efficiency, but also leverage. Creating this book allows me to leverage my knowledge to a greater extent, sharing it with tens of thousands of people, without an additional time spent. Throughout this book, you'll get a firm understanding of what exactly "leverage" really looks like.

Now, in the interest of saving time (since that is what we are all about with this course), let's get right to nuts and bolts, shall we?

For Further Research:

Instructor's Website:

http://jle.vi/

Follow Jonathan on Twitter:

http://twitter.com/entreprenewer

CHAPTER 2: STRUCTURE OF THIS COURSE

I know you are eager to get started, and of course, I want to be respectful and considerate of your time. So, just a quick explanation on how the book/course is structured.

In the Section 2, *General Principles & Theories For Hacking Your Productivity*, we are going to learn different overall strategies and theories around improving productivity. These general tips and tricks apply to every aspect of your life, not just the specific areas we upon which are going to focus. Investing in the right mindset and skill set is important in order to build the proper foundation for the subsequent productivity hacks. You should view the theories and strategies in Section 2 as ways of thinking, ways of looking at your work, and different "mental hacks" to improve your productivity, efficiency, and efficacy in any task you pursue.

In each of the next four sections, we are going to tackle an area of life where people typically spend a lot of their time. These include:

- ☐ Speeding Up and Automating Computer Work
- ☐ Speeding Up Health and Fitness
- ☐ Automating Your Finances
- ☐ Delegation and Saying "No"

By the way, we welcome and appreciate your requests and suggestions for other sections we can add and improve as time goes on.

In each of these overarching sections, we are going to check out a few strategies, tools, tricks, and tips we can use speed up or otherwise automate some time-consuming tasks. Some areas lend themselves more easily to improvements, and, therefore, there will be more resources for, say, something like computer work than there will be for sleep, which is a pretty fundamental biological need.

Anyway, if you are reading this book, it is safe to assume you are suffering from a lack of free time. Thus, in the interest of time and efficiency, my goal is **NOT** to give you a full crash course on any one subject or to make you a master of each individual topic or subject. Instead, I will give you an introduction, a contextual explanation, and help you understand where the concept or practice fits into the bigger picture.

Then, I will provide you some carefully curated supplementary materials, which you should read and digest as homework. I expect you, as a diligent student, will seek out further learning on topics **you** find interesting.

This coincides with my background in accelerated learning; I know that when you make the material your own, interact with and dig into the topics YOU are interested in on your own time, you really internalize the topic. Therefore, while we may go quickly, there is a reason!

A note on the computer stuff, by the way: For most demonstrations, I will be using a Mac, iPhone, or iPad; but do not worry - I will also give links, explanations, and examples (and often screenshots) for Windows, Android, and even Linux.

Last but not least, I want to say *not every hack is for everyone*. Some people *enjoy* the process of leisurely walking to work for 30 minutes when they could just as easily ride a bike in 5 minutes. I understand the choice, and so you need to pick and choose what is helpful to you and leave the rest alone for now. Who knows, you may find a need for different hacks at a future point in your life!

My fellow life hackers, now, without any further adieu (and thanks for your patience!), let's dive into our first section, which deals with the overall principles of speeding up and hacking productivity. This will give us the right mental framework and understanding to apply all the subsequent tricks, tips, and hacks.

CHAPTER 3: WHY DO THINGS QUICKER?

As I teach in my SuperLearning course, there are a couple key principles adult learners need to commit to and understand before we can really effectively learn anything. One main principle is the importance of understanding *why* we are learning a given skill or subject.

Beyond the importance of understanding *why*, we need to actually understand the practical application of our knowledge. In other words, we need to envision how we are actually going to *use* the knowledge we acquire. This simple fact is the reason why you probably do not remember trigonometry anymore. I sure don't.

These are just two of the six principles required for adult learning, but you can leave the other four to me for now, and be safe in the knowledge I have built these strategies into each one of my books.

In any case, these two principles are important enough to justify starting our course out with a little bit of a homework assignment. Do not worry, the homework is not too bothersome or time consuming.

I want you to write out at least three reasons **why** you want to become more efficient, productive, or quicker.

Get specific, though. Do not write something really elusive like "I want to have more time." Instead, maybe write something like, "I want to have an extra 3 hours a week to read to my kids so they will be ready to start first grade this fall," or, "I want to have an extra 2 hours a week to do Yoga so I can fix my knee pain and stress issues." Get really specific and explain *why* you want to save time.

Before you start, let me give you a little guidance from someone who is obsessed with efficiency and productivity. I *do not* improve my productivity or find life hacks because I want extra time to sit on my butt. I also do not necessarily improve productivity so I can do a superhuman workload, either.

Personally, I improve productivity so I can fill my life with other things which are meaningful and enjoyable, and which cannot, or should not, be optimized or hacked for efficiency, whether that is time with friends, playing sports I enjoy, or guilty pleasures like watching movies.

It is important that you do not have any illusions. Being more efficient does not necessarily mean you are more productive. After all, we all get exhausted, and there is a limit to how much you can reasonably do in a day.

Remember, while time is the most valuable and finite resource, time without attention is worthless. What I ask of you: do not use these skills to work yourself to death. Use them to make time for meaningful and enjoyable things in your life. If meaningful and enjoyable for you means working more, great - I have no problems with making that decision, personally. However, if gaining these skills is a means for spending time on meaningful and enjoyable things that *aren't* work, respect yourself enough to acknowledge that fact.

OK... with the touchy-feely part out of the way, the next mini assignment is to identify three to five areas where you feel you could save time. This will help in setting a goal and focus area for you, but it is also something interesting for me to understand as I improve the course in the future.

I have attached supplemental materials to this chapter which you may download and which will help guide you in further study (http://jle.vi/speedpdf).

One is a PDF syllabus with all the links and a layout of the course. You should download the syllabus as a great way to keep track of the many, many articles I will suggest. On that same page, you'll find a link to a Zip file of all the bookmarks, which you can import into your browser for fast access to articles, software, and other stuff I am going to recommend. Finally, there is a Facebook page and a Facebook group, which you should Like and Join respectively, so you can converse with others and share additional techniques and tactics which I have not covered.

So, you have some homework. Download, like, join, and then write out your reasons and areas of improvement. This is important. You can jot these down on your PDF syllabus, share them on the Facebook group, or do it old school and write your reasons on pen and paper. The choice is up to you, but make sure you complete the homework.

For Further Research:

Homework: Write out 3 reasons and 3-5 focus areas for speeding up and being more productive.

Syllabus:

http://jle.vi/speedpdf

Facebook:

https://www.facebook.com/groups/35218108 4960360/

HTML bookmarks file:

http://jle.vi/sdbookmarks

Chapter 4: Where Most People Spend (Or Waste) Their Time

Now, as with most people, you have some priority items you want to work on. Let's discuss where people spend and waste the most time. I (along with some other prominent thinkers) have identified a number of areas where time is wasted. This is not to say these activities are always a waste of time (though they definitely are sometimes), or they are inherently unimportant. When I say time is wasted on them, I am suggesting more time is invested on these activities than is necessary. It is in these areas we will make our biggest wins.

So, what are these things? Well, let me start with an example.

Have you ever sent an email to someone with a question or concern, only to receive a reply requiring further follow up? You are sending back and forth emails trying to understand each other, when perhaps a phone call would be more effective. The email "followup rat race" is a perfect (though very basic) example of time wasted, and this scenario happens every day, maybe even several times a day. We will get to email and communication later.

Of course, how we spend our time is highly variable for each person, and so giving you stats or averages like "the average American watches 2.2 hours of TV per day" or "the average sales professional spends 84 minutes a day on email" is both useless and meaningless. If you are interested, I have posted a link to a highly detailed and interactive breakdown by the

New York Times showing how different groups spend their time down to the nitty-gritty. Their research is absolutely fascinating, but not really important for progressing through the course. Instead, let me give you some more generic observations of some categories.

These types of "time wasters" do not correspond to the sections of the course; instead, each section will invariably have techniques for avoiding each of them. In any case, talking about time wasters is good because you start thinking about them in advance - this is another one of those learning philosophies I mentioned in Chapter 2.

So, how do we waste time?

First is *communication, scheduling, and planning with others* – basically, situations where our productivity or efficiency is dependent on someone else. This includes emails, texting, and other inefficiencies. Time wasters also include waiting 3 days for an email reply from your boss before starting work on a project.

The second is unnecessary effort or *doing things slowly or ineffectively*. A good example of this would be running on a treadmill for an hour and a half, when in fact you can generate the same health benefits in a properly designed 12-minute workout. Another example might be searching through folders on your computer for a file you need 3 times a day, or how about sleeping 8 hours when the last 30 minutes of sleep you are tossing and turning? You get the idea.

The next area where people waste time is in *ineffectively structuring or stacking tasks*. If you are the kind of person who folds one shirt at a time on the table, then turns around to put one folded shirt in the closet (instead of waiting until all the shirts are folded) – this is the kind of stuff we are going to try and eliminate. With different strategies and hacks, we are going to try and figure out how to make the most of our attention and effort by structuring our activities intelligently.

Finally, there is *the element of "choice"* and placing your efforts wisely on things you do well, and giving up on the rest. If you have ever met someone who insists on fixing his or her own car, even if it takes 6 hours and is not a perfect fix, this is the kind of stuff I am talking about here. We are going to talk about how to decide what is and is not an effective use of time, and how to be honest with yourself about how time is invested.

Hopefully, you see some of these elements in your day-to-day life, and you are both ready and excited to tackle them.

For Further Research:

New York Times: How Different Groups Spend Their Day:

http://jle.vi/spend

Chapter 5: Course Syllabus

If you haven't already, please take a moment to download the course syllabus:

http://jle.vi/speedpdf

The syllabus contains clickable links to supplemental material which are an important part of this book/course.

If you have not done so already, download the HTML bookmarks file. This is one of those productivity things – you have all the links in one place so you do not spend time searching for them!

http://jle.vi/sdbookmarks

Also, remember to like and join the Facebook group and participate in the discussions.

http://jle.vi/speeddemonsgroup

I know, I've asked for a lot of "out of the book" activities. That's why, if you head to the download page above, I've given you an opportunity to get a free video interview with one of the world's top productivity gurus, Chris Bailey. Think of it as a reward for taking action and being active in your learning process.

SECTION 2: GENERAL PRINCIPLES & THEORIES FOR HACKING YOUR PRODUCTIVITY

Chapter 6: The Power Of Preparation

For part of her career, my mother was a highly skilled seamstress creating beautiful and eloquent costumes for children's theatre productions. I was always amazed by how she managed to get something done in half the time it would have taken another seamstress, without any apparent reduction in quality.

When I asked my mom how she was so effective at her work, she simply replied, "I measure twice, and cut once." This is really similar to the legendary quote by Abraham Lincoln, "Give me six hours to chop down a tree, and I will spend the first four sharpening the axe."

Now, I do not want to get into a long and drawn out lecture about the importance of preparation. So instead, I will say this. Whether you are learning a new skill, writing an article, or cutting down a tree, the old adage is true: a minute of preparation saves an hour of deliberation. We all fall prey to improper preparation.

In fact, as I wrote out my talking points for this exact lecture in the original course, I realized I needed to look up the exact Abraham Lincoln quote. Looking up the quote meant switching gears, searching through Google, and losing my focus. If I had searched for all the quotes ahead of time and had them ready alongside my text-editing app, I would have saved at least 5 minutes.

Of course, nobody is perfect, and remembering to invest in proper preparation is an ongoing battle for me. But first and foremost, I want to alert you to the fact you can save a LOT of time by properly preparing. We will explain this a bit more when we get into the power of maintaining concentration and the unforeseen perils of distractions.

This applies to almost anything you do in life. If you are writing a research paper, pull up all the articles beforehand so you do not have to break your concentration to search for them.

If you are cooking, pull all the ingredients out of the fridge, take them out of the plastic bags, and put them in your work area in an organized manner.

If you are fixing a car, figure out what size bolts the car uses and organize all of the tools you will need in advance.

If you are heading into a meeting, brief yourself on the other person's credentials so you can avoid asking unnecessary clarification questions or asking those resumé questions nobody likes to answer.

You get the idea.

Invest in your preparation up front, and you can save tons of time in execution - and we have not even gotten into strategies for being more effective in the tasks themselves!

CHAPTER 7: HAVING CLEAR PRIORITIES AND GOALS AND MAKE THEM SMART

I know, I know, the following does not sound like a productivity hack, but trust me, it is. Having clear priorities helps us place our efforts intelligently. Have you ever sat down to answer a bunch of emails, and then found a Software Update email in one of them? Of course, you do not want to forget to update a critical piece of software, and so you click the link. But then you have to close all your windows, update another piece of software the first update requires, back up your files... now, you've lost 30 minutes of time that *should* have gone to your important emails.

Setting priorities helps us be responsible and accountable to ourselves. But, not all goals and priorities are created equal. In fact, there is a theory around what criteria each goal, priority, or task should incorporate. This methodology is called SMART, and it was originally a methodology managers used to get better performance from their employees. However, the same methodology is just as relevant for helping us manage *ourselves*.

SMART is an acronym:

Specific
Measurable
Assignable
Realistic
Time-Related

If we are using this for ourselves and not employees, we can convert the A from Assignable into "Ambitious" or "Actionable," depending on the goal.

The rest of the acronym is pretty self-explanatory, and I do not want to waste your precious time with the details of what each one really means, or the alternate definitions. For the details, I have linked you to the Wikipedia article where you can read all about SMART if you want. Instead, I will demonstrate by giving you an example of a lousy priority or goal, and an example of a "SMART" one.

Right now, I am working on learning Russian. I have set myself a goal to learn Russian and made it a priority in my life. But, if I say "Improve Russian Skills," measurement becomes hard to quantify; how do I know if I have accomplished the goal or not?

How much is enough? By when? What does improvement really mean - does improvement mean repeating the same sentences with better pronunciation, or is improvement being able to recite Pushkin?

Instead, I have written down the following goal: By December 31, I will be able to hold at least a 5-minute conversation about common everyday topics such as introductions, weather, or personal interests with a native Russian speaker, without reverting to English.

This goal is specific, because I know exactly what topics I will need to learn. The goal is also measurable – if I can only last 4 minutes before resorting to English, I will have failed. The goal is Ambitious, because Russian is very difficult, and right now I can only converse about 1 minute without reverting to English. The goal is Realistic, though, because I was able to acquire the first minute with only 30-40 hours of work. And of course, because I have set a date (December 31), it is Time-Related.

Anyways, setting these clear goals and priorities helps me know where best to invest my efforts. I am not working on improving my professional vocabulary, and

I am avoiding the temptation to improve my Spanish or Hebrew skills, because those goals are not the priority at hand.

However, what about managing smaller tasks, priorities, and goals that take hours, not months? Well, it is important to write them down and create accurate to-do-lists. One popular book about effective strategies for using and making to-do-lists is the Checklist Manifesto, which I will link in the supplementary materials. Furthermore, I have my own strategy and software stack for task prioritization which works quite well. If you are like me, you have a task management software for work that helps you coordinate with your colleagues - something like Basecamp, Podio, or my personal favorite, Asana. I definitely recommend you use some kind of software or app that lets you input To-Do's and set deadlines for them. However, you probably also use some different kind of personal to-do list – the one that comes on your iPhone, or Evernote, or something like Wunderlist. (Do not worry, I will provide links to my top recommended ones in the supplementary materials).

The thing is, with all these different apps being used for different purposes, how the heck are you supposed to prioritize tasks when they are all over the place? The task reminding you to pick up your dry cleaning is in a totally different software or website than the task reminding you to update the company website, for example.

Well, there is a great app called TacoApp which solves this exact problem. TacoApp connects to practically every task management software or to-do list out there, and imports all of your tasks. It then gives you one clean interface, where you can sort your tasks onto the main dashboard and prioritize them across different fields. As you see, I can sort different tasks whether they are for the startup I work with, courses I am working on, or my personal to-do's. TacoApp also updates the various apps when you mark something complete, and sends you a daily "punch list" every morning so you do not get distracted by a long, scary sidebar of tasks.

Personally, I love the fact I can ask Siri or OK Google, "Remind me to pick up my dry-cleaning tomorrow at noon," and that ends up alongside my tasks for work, allowing me to prioritize whether I will fix the company website before or after picking up the dry cleaning. Check out TacoApp and see if it is a good fit for you.

In conclusion, setting well-designed goals and priorities helps us be accountable to ourselves; if you have a SMART goal to accurately and politely answer all 27 emails from your colleagues *before* lunch at 12:30, you are going to have a much harder time procrastinating by checking Facebook, getting up for an extra cup of coffee, and so on. In fact, that is a perfect segue into our next chapter, which talks about the importance of deadlines.

For Further Research:

TacoApp:

http://jle.vi/tacoapp

SMART Criteria Wikipedia:

http://jle.vi/smartcriteria

Five Best ToDo List Managers – Lifehacker:

http://jle.vi/to-dolistmanagers

Asana:

http://jle.vi/asana

The CheckList Manifesto Amazon:

http://jle.vi/thechecklistmanifesto1

The CheckList Manifesto iTunes:

http://jle.vi/thechecklistmanifesto2

CHAPTER 8: ORGANIZING PRIORITIES WITH THE PRIORITY STAR EXERCISE

In this book, I talk about how prior planning is really important - and that's definitely true. If we know what we need to do, and we have our priorities outlined clearly, it will basically set us up for success. There's no losing of focus or going off task to try and understand what we need to be doing next.

One exercise that I really love for prioritization is called the priority Star exercise. This is a great exercise that helps you take 5 to do items that are loosely interrelated, and structure them in step-by-step processes. In order to illustrate the power of this, I am going to actually use a real-life example. About a year ago, I was working on establishing a new blog called Becoming SuperHuman.

Real life example: my new blog project
http://becomingasuperhuman.com

I had a lot of work to do for setting up this blog. There's a lot of different aspects and a lot of different moving parts. Let me tell you what 5 of them are.

First of all I wanted to launch with a lot of blog posts.

I wanted to do a podcast with great audio interviews and cool stuff like that. The next thing would therefore be to establish a podcast - denoted in the image below as "PC."

Of course, I was also going to need to set up an email list so that people could subscribe. Let's call that "email lists."

Of course, I needed to pick a domain name get all the domain and Web server stuff set up.

Notice in the diagram below that I've arranged these in a Pentagon. There is a reason for that.

The last thing is I needed to decide on was a design. That design goes for the logo, which fortunately I had already done early on, but also a nice design for the web site.

So, as you see below, I have my pentagon of five interrelated tasks that I needed to get done before I could launch my new blog.

Now: Let's go ahead and go through the exercise. The idea is that if you look at all five of these tasks, it's really hard to think about what we should do first. Maybe domain setup will jump out at you. What about the other ones? Should I record podcasts before I do the posts? Should I set up the email list before I set up the design?

Of course, this isn't a perfect example, because perhaps for those of you who have set up web sites, the answer is really clear. On the other hand, it's a great example, because all these things are interrelated. They are all aspects of one project.

So, here's how it works. I need to think about the interrelation between each one. I usually start at the top. So let's start at Posts. I ask myself a simple question: Will writing posts help power the podcast, or will creating the podcast help power new posts?

Posts

PC

Design

Interconnect each possible pair
Draw an arrow showing which item will help or drive which

Eml List

Well, it actually turns out that that the podcasts will *be* posts on the site, and so for every podcast I create, that's a post. Setting up a podcast is going to actually drive posts.

Now the next one, Posts to email lists: Are people going to sign up for my email list if I don't have any posts? Probably not. So I think that having posts is going to drive the success of the email list.

What about the relation between posts and a domain name and my web server? Well, I can't really work on anything until I have the domain name set up. So the domain name is going to drive the posts.

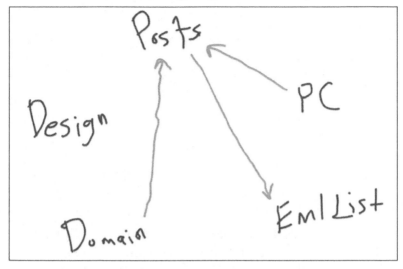

What about Posts and design? Well this one is tricky, because realistically, I could write some posts and schedule them before I have my design. But actually, if you think about it, the size of my images that I put in my post and all that stuff is going to depend on the design. So actually, I should probably have my designs set up and know what my aesthetic is going to look like before I do the posts. So design will drive the success of the posts.

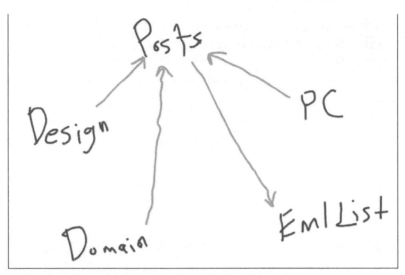

Now let's go to the podcasts over on the right side. Will having a podcast improve the success of my emails, or will having an email list improve the success of my podcast? Well, if I have the podcast, that's more material, and more material means it will appeal to more people... so probably, having my podcasts set up drives my email list. But let's think about it the other of the way. If I have my email list, will it help me get more interviewees for my podcast? Probably not. I can safely say that having a podcast will make the email list more successful.

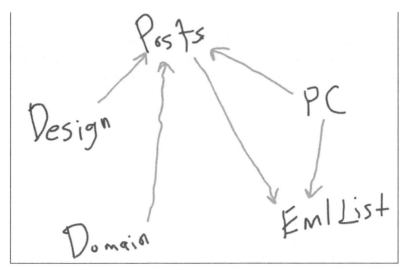

What about the relationship between the podcast and a domain? Well really I would say that in the podcast, I'm probably going to have to talk about the domain, how you can download the notes from this podcast at www.BecomingASuperHuman.com. So really, having the domain name setup is going to make the podcast possible.

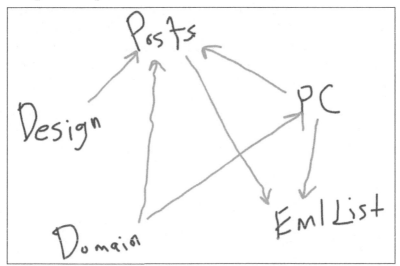

Now, what about the podcast and the design? I guess they are not really related unless my podcast image is supposed to match my design, and when I submit it to iTunes, I need to have a graphic... so really, I guess I need my design to be all set up before I really launch the podcasts.

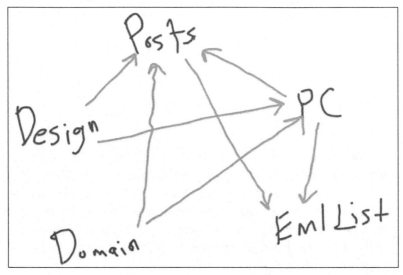

Now, going back down to email lists: Does having an email list make the domain more successful? No, it turns out I need to know what my domain name is and I need to have my email server set up before I can make the email list a reality.

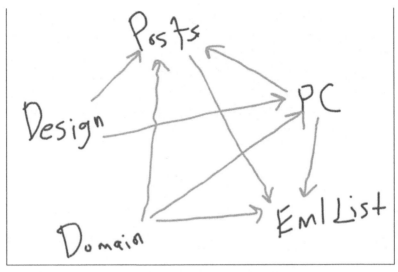

What about the email list and design? Well my emails are going to have to match the design of my web site, so I better decide on that before I set up the email list.

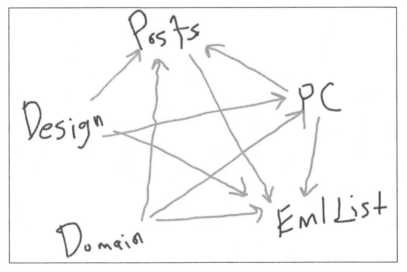

Now just wrapping up, let's look at the domain and the design. I definitely could do them separately, and sometimes you will find tasks that you can argue either way for. In that instance, I just have to make a decision either way. I guess it's going to be a lot easier to do my design work once I have a domain name and I can do the logo. I need to decide on my domain name first, because it will go into my logo and of course I am able to preview it and send it to friends. So I better have my server and my domain set up before I do my design.

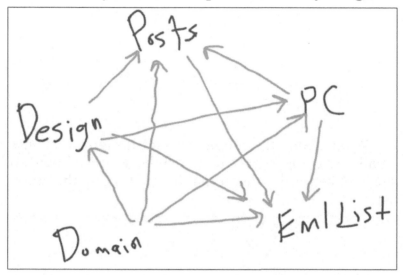

Now, you see we have nice little star up in the middle and all of them are connected around the outside of the pentagon. So that is perfect. That means we did the job well.

Now, how do we prioritize these tasks? Well it's really simple. We just need to count the number of *originating* arrows from each one.

Let's go around and count them. Posts and setting up the blog has just one originating arrow. So that's a 1.

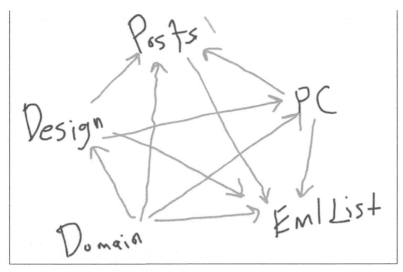

Podcast has 2 originating arrows. Email list has no originating arrows. Domain has 4, and design has 3 originating arrows.

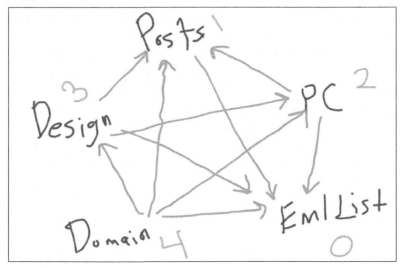

So basically, we now know our priorities - and I will tell you how. The number of originating arrows means that that item is critical for other items. So domain, with the highest number of originating arrows, means that this is priority No. 1.

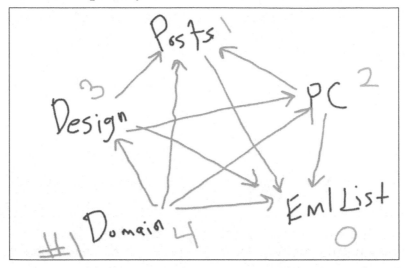

Design actually is going to be priority No. 2. So you might think that's surprising. Maybe I should write posts first, but in fact, the graph doesn't lie.

Now about the podcast - this really surprises me. I would think that I would write some posts before, but actually it shows above that the podcast should actually be priority No. 3. If I think about it intuitively the way I thought about it in this connection, it does make sense, because having the podcast set up and running is going to contribute to more posts, and post is priority No. 4.

Lastly, it turns out that the email list is the last thing I should worry about, which is really interesting, because I've been stressing out about this email list and getting it set up before I do anything. But in reality, the graph helps us understand that people are not going to subscribe until all these other things are set up and running, because there is no reason to subscribe if there are no posts, and the posts are driven by the podcast, and so on and so forth.

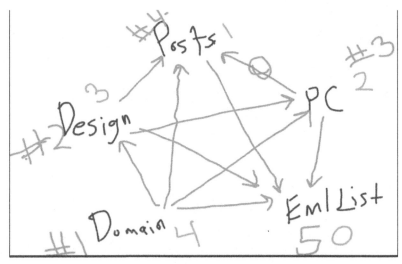

This is a really powerful framework for determining the priority of different tasks, and in which order you should do them. I sometimes use it for personal tasks that I need to coordinate in my own life, or for different professional projects. The key is that they need to be interrelated, and you need to think objectively about the different roles and interrelations between each task. So give it a try.

For Further Research:

Homework: Try the priority star exercise for 5 of your own tasks.

CHAPTER 9: SETTING DEADLINES, AND MAKING THEM REAL

For any of you who have read *The Four Hour Work Week* by Tim Ferriss, you are already familiar with the idea of Parkinson's Law. For those of you who have not, I strongly, strongly recommend reading the book and have a link in the supplemental materials. *The Four Hour Work Week* is an essential handbook on productivity and efficiency, and this course is heavily influenced by Tim's teachings, combined with my own tricks and tips for implementing them.

In any case, Parkinson's Law is the idea that work expands to fill the time allotted. When we feel we have all the time in the world, work drags on and expands. We decide to add more details, to triple-check unnecessarily, and so on. In reality, our brains are extremely effective at synthesizing what is and is not important – especially when we are in a rush or under pressure. If you were ever the student who waited until the last day of the semester to write your term paper, and accomplished weeks' worth of work in an evening, then you have experienced Parkinson's Law. In fact, many people are baffled to find they do their best, most productive work in spurts like this.

If this is true, then why not "hack" the psychological force behind Parkinson's Law? Why not set artificial deadlines for how long we will allow things to take? After all, we have all had days where we hardly manage to finish a few hours' worth of work by 5PM, while paradoxically we finish an entire day's worth of work when we have to leave early.

Personally, I have found setting "artificial" deadlines to be quite difficult, because deep down, I know they are fake and meaningless. I read about Parkinson's Law years and years ago in *The Four Hour Work Week*, and failed to implement Parkinson's Law, until I discovered my own hack – making the deadlines real. When I know I can "push back" the deadline, I usually do, and then work will expand once again. However, if I have a Skype call, a meeting, or a doctor's appointment, there is no pushing those activities back. As an example, as I wrote the first draft of this chapter, I was rushing against the clock, knowing I had an appointment only half an hour away. I decided I *had* to write out my rough drafts for all of the chapters through Section 2 before leaving, because I scheduled my day in such a way that I would not have time after my appointment. I simply could not believe how productive I was!

I use this hack all the time; I find the pressure of being late and the unpleasantness of leaving a task incomplete is highly effective for me. I bet that throughout the day there are dozens of things you simply *cannot* push back: picking the kids up from school, a meeting with your boss, and so on. When those things happen, and you have small blocks of time, pick a task that should take twice as long, and try to sandwich it in. Worst case, your work quality is not good enough and you have to revisit the task... but even if you have to tweak the quality (and the quality probably will not need tweaking), the surge of productivity will be astonishing, and you can always apply a deadline to the revision work, too.

Play around with Parkinson's Law and set some deadlines for work that drags on and on, and see how you progress. You will probably cut some corners – but those corners probably will not be important or worth the time they would take. In fact, the majority of the "details" in reality are not important in a lot of tasks – and those "details" are the subject of our next chapter, on the Pareto Principle.

For Further Research:

The 4Hour Workweek Amazon:

http://jle.vi/4hww

The Four Hour Work Week iTunes

http://jle.vi/4hww2

Parkinson's Law Wikipedia

http://jle.vi/parkinsonslaw

CHAPTER 10: THE PARETO PRINCIPLE: OUR SECRET TO BEING EFFECTIVE

At this point in the course, the difference between being *efficient* and being *effective* is extremely important to make clear. You can be extremely *efficient* at a task; however, if the task is meaningless (say ironing socks), then the task of ironing socks does not make you any more *effective* at doing your laundry. In order to be both efficient *and* effective, we need to understand which elements of the priority or task actually contribute to the quality or desirability of the outcome – right?

Here's another great tip I owe to Timothy Ferriss; if you've already read some of his work or are familiar with this particular principle, I apologize for the repetition, but the tip is important enough to deserve a review.

Tim is a big believer in something called the Pareto Principle, or the 80/20 rule. The rule is named after Italian economist Vilfredo Pareto, who made an observation in 1906 that 80% of the land in Italy was owned by 20% of the population. He further developed the principle by observing 20% of the pea pods in his garden contained 80% of the peas.

Okay, maybe observing peas is probably not very interesting. But the applications born out of the 80/20 rule and the subsequent 90/10 rule are *really* important.

For example, in my former business, I did some analysis and realized 80% of my customers gave me only 20% of my revenues. By focusing on the *other* 20%

of my customers, who gave me 80% of my revenues, I was able to be much more effective in my goal to grow my business and turn a healthy profit. As a side note, I also realized 20% of my customers gave me 80% of the headaches, and I made sure to recommend those customers check out my competitor's website!

Pareto's law has a limitless number of applications, but here are a few to think about:

Roughly 20% of the words in most languages make up 80% of conversations: start by learning those words!

Roughly 20% of the work of cooking makes 80% of the difference in how tasty the food is – why do the other 80% of the work?!

Probably 80% of the news articles you read only give you 20% new information – why waste your time reading those extra articles?

Probably less than 20% of the people you would call friends or family make up 80% of your happiness, support, and enjoyment – focus your attention and time on those people!

In fact, I bet 20% of the tips I give you in this course will make up 80% of the value you extract from the course personally – but hold on a minute, that does not mean you should start skipping sections!

This one point is the principle behind most of Tim Ferriss' success in business, writing, investing, and learning new skills. He is a master of deconstructing a subject and figuring out what he calls the "minimum effective dose" for success. While you can view this as doing the bare minimum, and certainly the bare minimum is not appropriate for everything, the principle can have massive implications on how effective you are, and subsequently, how efficient.

So, your "homework," if you can call it homework, is to start viewing the world through the lens of 80/20.

When you catch yourself sitting through a boring meeting or writing an email, I want you to think, "If I could remove 80% of this, what parts would remain?" Though we cannot always do this, especially with meetings, a good practice is to start thinking in this way, and the practice will help us immensely when we take a big machete to our workflows and start cutting things.

For Further Research:

Pareto principle Wikipedia:

http://jle.vi/paretoprinciple

Homework: Think about Pareto Principle & How to apply it

Chapter 11: The "Bad" Kind of Multitasking, Avoiding Distractions, and Meditation

You might think, because this is a course on productivity hacking, I am going to teach you how to do 10 things at once to speed things up. In fact, this is not true at all. While the next chapter will deal with how to use multitasking effectively and responsibly, I want to impress upon you that 80% of multitasking is in fact destructive to your productivity and work quality.

You can probably make assumptions about the effects of multitasking on focus, and you likely know that dividing your attention across three tasks has a high cost in terms of efficiency and work output. No surprises there. But did you know that when switching between micro-tasks, there is a distinct period of confusion before you can re-enter into the focused state? We are going to talk about this more in an upcoming chapter about focus and flow, but for now, I want to give you an example you have probably experienced.

Imagine you are filling out a work-related form, and you are fully focused. You are "in the zone" – until someone calls you on the phone. This has surely happened to you, and so you have experienced the feeling of settling back down after the phone call and trying to figure out where you were on the form. Picking up where you left off may seem like only a few seconds, but if you are performing some kind of high-functioning task, in fact "picking up" takes much longer. In fact, it is been suggested that "picking back up" can take as much as 15 minutes to get back into the "zone." This is to say that while our brains are very sophisticated at maintaining up to 9 of different threads of thoughts or focus at once, the brain is far less efficient at doing so than we would like to believe.

While you may pride yourself on being able to listen to a podcast, answer chat messages from customers, read your emails, and chit chat with your coworker across the room, the reality is each and every "micro" shift is costing you productivity. The "cost" may mean re-reading the chat message from a minute ago, asking your coworker to repeat something they said, or to rewind the podcast a little bit. Those little "hiccups" add up and cost you time! Not to mention, the quality of your work is not nearly as good.

Instead, I would encourage you to shut off all distractions, whenever possible. Try to do one thing at a time, and only one thing. If your coworkers want to chat, put the emails on hold. If you are answering emails, set yourself a deadline (like we discussed earlier), and put on headphones with some non-distracting music to make it clear to other people present that you are focusing. Then, set your phone to "do not disturb," and get the emails done. For activities requiring your mental acuity, multitasking is about the worst thing you can do for productivity.

Give this a try – stay focused on one task and see how much more effective you are. You might find staying focused is really hard for you (especially if your brain has learned to love jumping around). I found this to be true when I started meditating.

By the way, meditation is a really great practice to get into, because meditation helps us train our brains to focus on one thing at a time and helps us understand how impossible maintaining singular focus has become in our culture of constant multi-sensory overload. If you decide to embark on a journey of meditation (which I strongly recommend), you might be shocked and disappointed to see you can only focus on something as simple as your breath for 1 or 2 seconds before getting distracted. The beauty of meditation is that it simultaneously teaches you to improve your focus while training you to accept the "monkey mind" and avoid aggravation.

In fact, a great majority of the world's most productive and successful people in the arts, business, government, and more are all avid practitioners of meditation, from Oprah to Tony Robbins to Bill Clinton and even Paul McCartney. There are literally thousands of top-performers who claim a huge part of their success is owed to the focus they gained from meditation. Therefore, I strongly recommend you check out some of the links I have provided.

Meditation is a surprisingly difficult thing to do, and I know, most of you will say "I am just not someone who can meditate," but trust me, meditation is well, well worth the effort, if you are willing to tough out the learning curve!

In the next chapter, I am going to talk about how to properly stack activities, now that you understand why micro switching of tasks is counter-productive.

For Further Research:

Benefits of Meditation

http://jle.vi/meditation1

What Happens to the Brain When You Meditate

http://jle.vi/meditation2

Media Multitaskers Pay a Mental Price – Stanford Research

http://jle.vi/multitask1

The Science Behind MultiTasking – From an MIT Researcher

http://jle.vi/multitask3

Why the Human Brain Can't MultiTask – TEDx

http://jle.vi/multitask4

The Illusion of MultiTasking – UCSD Center for Mindfulness

http://jle.vi/multitask5

How (and Why) to Stop Multitasking – Harvard Business Review

http://jle.vi/multitask6

Chapter 12: Batching Similar Tasks

So, now we have an understanding of how crucial it is to avoid the confusion and disorientation of switching between tasks or threads, let's add the fact that there is an inherent amount of "setup" for each task. For example, you wouldn't put on your workout clothes, stretch out, do 20 pushups, shower, get changed, and then repeat the process a few hours later to do your 20 squats... would you? Of course not! Doing so would be a ridiculous waste of time, and so you do the pushups and the squats (and hopefully some other exercises) all at the same time.

So, why do you do this with email? Or, for that matter, why do you do it with any kind of task? We probably do not think about batching similar tasks. However, batching allows us to amortize, or divide, the setup and recovery time involved with those tasks across more items.

Since we have already learned how important "preparation" is, doing preparation more than one time is a huge shame. Also, since we have talked about the hidden cost of mentally switching tasks, we now understand why batching tasks is so important.

Your homework is to try batching simple tasks, like answering email only twice a day at specific times. If you cannot manage to do that (do not worry, neither can I), then you should try to put all of your errands, like picking up the kids from school and buying groceries, in the same trip. If you start looking at batching tasks, there will be a lot of tasks you can batch together for optimal efficiency. You just have to look to find the low-hanging fruit.

For Further Research:

Homework: Try batching similar tasks in your daily life

CHAPTER 13: THE "GOOD" KIND OF MULTITASKING AND THE WHEEL OF LIFE

So, while 80% of multitasking is honestly pretty awful, there is, as always, 20% that is actually quite useful. To explain what I mean, I have to go on a bit of a tangent, though.

Early on in my career, I was exposed to an idea called "The Wheel of Life." This is a circle with 8 sections to represent how satisfied or successful you feel you are with different aspects of your life, such as Friends and Family, Personal Growth, Health, Finances, etc. Satisfaction and success are a whole set of different subjects for a different course, and so I will give you a link to explore "The Wheel of Life" on your own time. However, I wanted to introduce this concept, because learning about the wheel of life introduced me to another idea.

You might be relieved to know that you can actually accomplish 2 goals at once by doing *mutually productive* activities. The idea here is to never do an activity which does not improve your progress in *at least* 2 sections of the wheel of life.

This is a bit confusing. It may seem too analytical, and it is hard to explain theoretically, so let me give you some examples in my own personal life.

One of my goals, as I mentioned, is to improve my Russian Language skills. Now, I could hire a tutor, sure, but that would only accomplish one goal. The tutor would only improve one section of my "wheel of life" - Personal Growth. However, if I decide to travel to Russia and practice with native speakers there, as I have done twice this year, then my satisfaction in the "fun and adventure" category are also improved, while simultaneously improving my Russian skills. Even better, if I decide to visit my friends from business school while I am in Russia, that makes 3 sections all being mutually fulfilled!

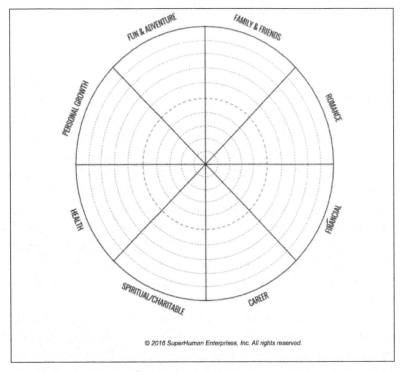

It gets better than that, actually, because some activities are *even better* if done in conjunction with one another. Here are a few examples:

Learning to speak Russian in a higher-stakes environment, with native speakers in Russia, is way more effective than learning from a textbook or tutor.

Double dates with friends or going to a museum and learning something new with your wife, boyfriend, girlfriend, etc. will improve your relationship more than sitting on the couch and watching movies together.

Exercising while learning or reading actually improves your memory and brain function.

Listening to an interesting podcast or audiobook can keep you alert and engaged while cooking or folding laundry

For these reasons, if you want to be really productive and effective, you should try to nurture 2 aspects of the circle at once. But hey, even I get tired and lazy sometimes. I watch TV and silly movies on the couch by myself every so often. But I can make a choice. If I am going to relax, I need to do *something* productive. For example, I can stretch out my muscles, because one of my goals is to improve my flexibility. I can watch the movie in Spanish or Hebrew, languages I want to improve.

The point is, you can always find ways to make even your "down time" productive in some way shape or form, ways in which are not exhausting or emotionally draining at all.

Try this out. I'm such a big advocate of the Wheel of Life, I actually use it to guide my entire goal-making and life planning regimen - and I encourage you to do the same. For this reason, I'm including a powerful worksheet, taken from my MasterClass, which you can download for free. Check i tout, and see how you can "link up" activities that are mutually productive or made better by the combination. Go for a run with a good friend instead of just you and the dog. Try reading while you are on the exercise bike. In short, figure out little ways you can use the "good" kind of multitasking to your benefit and make the most of your time.

For Further Research:

Wheel of Life Exercise (from the MasterClass)

http://jle.vi/wole

How exercise can help us learn – New York Times

http://jle.vi/exercise1

Research on Physical Exercise during Encoding of New Languages

http://jle.vi/exercise2

CHAPTER 14: PLANNING FOR STRUCTURED REST PERIODS

In the late 1980's, a university student named Francisco Cirillo figured out a neat little hack that made him more productive. Cirillo realized if he worked in blocks of 25 minutes, with short breaks in between, he was actually more productive than if he worked for blocks of 2 or 3 hours uninterrupted. He called this method the "Pomodoro" technique, because he used one of those little Tomato timers, or "Pomodori" in Italian.

This might seem contradictory to everything we said about batching tasks, avoiding distractions, setting deadlines, and so on - but it is not. You see, 25 minutes is not the critical part here, and obviously if you are fully focused or "in the zone," you can and should skip a break. What is critical is the process of planning breaks into your work schedule. For one, this actually helps us set artificial deadlines, because we know in whatever time period we specify, whether it is 25 minutes or an hour, we will have to take a break, and we do not want to be caught in the middle of the task. Second, because of the nature of the pomodori, or time periods, we have to do proper preparation and break the task into manageable chunks. This requires we estimate how much time each section will take, which requires some level of planning and macro-analysis, which helps set us up mentally for success and efficacy.

Also important is to note there are a lot of psychological effects involved in taking a break – if the break is planned and not a random interruption by a coworker or a text message. Perhaps you have experienced a situation in which you struggled with a math problem or a computer programming glitch, got frustrated, got up, took a break, came back, and solved the problem almost instantaneously? This is because a refreshed mind *is* much more effective, and these breaks enable the brain to look at things from a different viewpoint. You might not realize it, but our brains actually do a LOT of subconscious processing and digestion when we are not working on the task itself.

Have you ever heard someone say they do their best thinking in the shower, away from the computer? Or a business executive who says he does his best work on the golf course?

Now you know why.

This is the case with the Pomodoro technique, too. The breaks not only refresh and relax us, force us to plan our work, set deadlines, be strategic and effective, but they also enable the brain to "do its thing," so to speak. The brain's "thing" is to process and digest the information with which we are interacting.

This is why, in my SuperLearning course, I recommend students to take a 1-2 second pause between pages, and as much as a 15-60 second break between chapters. I even recommend to close the book, process what they have just read, and maybe even walk away. This is a highly effective technique for letting the brain do all its "background activity."

So, check out the Wikipedia article on the Pomodoro technique, experiment with different time intervals, and try building in timely, automatic breaks between your tasks. Like I said, if you are "in the zone" − something I will be talking about at the end of this section − you should definitely skip breaks.

Otherwise, you will likely find a ton of benefits from the breaks. I would be lying if I said I know exactly how Pomodoro works, but believe me, it does!

For Further Research:

Pomodoro Technique Illustrated – Amazon

http://jle.vi/pomodoro1

Pomodoro Technique – Wikipedia

http://jle.vi/pomodoro2

CHAPTER 15: USING SMALL CHUNKS OF WASTED TIME EFFECTIVELY

We all have little periods of time throughout our day that go to waste because of circumstance. Usually, these chunks of time are spent waiting for something - standing at the bus stop, sitting in the back of a taxi, arriving early to a meeting, and so on. These chunks of time *usually* get filled with unproductive activities - we check Facebook, play Candy Crush, or some other mindless activity to pass the time. However, they really do not have to - if we do a little bit of planning and preparation.

Of course, in the moment, when we realize we may have 5-10 minutes of waiting, thinking of what we could do with the time is impossible. We default to whatever is easy and convenient. However, we ALL have those little "10 minute" tasks we do not have time to do, like calling Grandma, reviewing our flashcards, or reading the news. If you are like me, you push those tasks back because every time you sit down to get things done, they seem like they are not huge priorities.

The trick to actually *doing* these things during our gap time is to remove the elements of thinking and deliberation. Just make a list of things you will do when you have 5-10 minutes. It is important they are 5-10 minute chunks, so you can do at least one, but maybe 2 or 3 if you have a long taxi ride or the doctor is behind schedule. This is literally FREE productivity, time taken away from usually meaningless tasks.

Here are some of my personal "mini tasks" I do when I find myself stuck waiting for something:

Review Russian, Spanish, or Hebrew flash cards (this one is great, because I can do 1 minute or 1 hour, and it does not matter if I stop in the middle)

Call a friend or family member I have not spoken to in a while (to make this a no-brainer decision, I have a group on my address book of people I want to be in touch with)

Stretch out my muscles (if doing so is socially appropriate - and sometimes when it isn't)

Watch a lecture of whichever Udemy course I am currently taking (since they are usually 1-5 minutes and available on my phone)

By doing this, I accomplish lots of small stuff which would normally get pushed back, and because I am already "in between" tasks, such as getting out of the taxi and going into my meeting, I do not have to really break my concentration. I just sandwich something productive in between.

Try out these "mini tasks" and share in the Facebook group some of your "in between" tasks with others!

For Further Research:

Homework: Make a list of 5 to 10-minute tasks you can do in wasted chucks of time.

Chapter 16: A Brief Note On Flow And Focus

In the final "general principles" chapter before diving into the nuts-and-bolts techniques, I want to talk about perhaps the most important aspect of productivity: *focus*. As I mentioned earlier in the course, time is very valuable, but time without attention is practically worthless. I have also talked a lot about being "in the zone" and knowing when to skip taking breaks.

It is important for us to know when we are and are not focused. If you cannot sit at your desk and work right now, maybe you should tackle another task, like exercising.

In fact, I want to talk about "focus" a bit more scientifically, though not on the level of neurologists or psychologists, by introducing the flow state. **Flow**, or what I have been referring to as being "in the zone," is defined as the *mental state of operation* in which a person performing an activity is fully immersed in a feeling of energized focus, full involvement, and enjoyment in the process of the activity. Basically, flow is characterized by complete absorption in what one does.

This is important because it relates to everything we have taught thus far. You see, it is reasonable to assume 80% of the important work you do is done in the 20% of time you are in the flow state, hyper focused and on the ball. In fact, if you think back to the example where I asked if you had ever done an entire term paper the day before an exam, this was possible because the sense of urgency (or doom) pushed you into the flow state.

You should be aware of this, and of course, you should try to do as much of your work as possible in flow. You should also try to get into flow as much as possible; however, that could be the subject of an entirely different course and in fact, entire books have been written on this topic alone. To save you lots of research, here are 7 conditions to flow proposed by recent research:

1. Knowing what to do
2. Knowing how to do it
3. Knowing how well you are doing
4. Knowing where to go (if navigation is involved)
5. High-perceived challenges
6. High-perceived skills
7. Freedom from distractions

It probably does not take much for you to understand how the other strategies outlined in this section (preparation, SMART goals, Pareto's Law, Parkinson's Law, Pomodoro time, avoiding the wrong kinds of multitasking, etc.) are all closely related to flow. By preparing ourselves so we know what to do, preparing our environment to be free of distractions, creating high challenges on our time and challenging goals, we maximize the likelihood of entering flow, and therefore maximize the likelihood of kicking butt.

I have added some great additional resources including a TED talk and a Wikipedia article discussing flow as being the key to success and happiness. I encourage you to read up on *flow*.

I will not say more on *overall* principles and strategies of efficiency, efficacy, and speeding things up. We have come a long way! It may seem like a lot of philosophical principles and "fluff" before the "juicy stuff," but I can tell you that if there really is 20% of the course that makes up 80% of the benefit, at least half of it is contained in the previous few chapters. These are the fundamentals, the foundations to productivity and efficacy.

Take time to understand the principles, read the supplementary materials describing them, think about how they apply to your daily life, and see where they might fit into your workflow before we move on.

For Further Research:

Flow (psychology) – Wikipedia

http://jle.vi/flow1

Mihaly Csikszentmihalyi: Flow, the secret to happiness – TED

http://jle.vi/flow2

What Is Flow? – The Psychology of Flow

http://jle.vi/flow3

SECTION 3: SPEEDING UP & AUTOMATING COMPUTER WORK

CHAPTER 17: JUST HOW MUCH TIME ARE YOU WASTING ON YOUR COMPUTER?

Before we tackle the subject of computer / digital productivity, it is worthwhile to start setting some baselines. As the old adage goes, what gets measured gets done. By measuring how productive (or unproductive) we are, only then do we can truly realize gains.

I, for one, was shocked to find out my little "Pomodoro technique" breaks viewing funny internet memes were not costing me a handful of chunks of 5 minutes per day. In reality they were costing me, on average, over an hour a day! How did I measure this in order to keep myself accountable and correct the problem?

Enter RescueTime. RescueTime is a really cool cross-platform application you can install on your Mac, PC, Linux machine, Android phone, and more. The app sits on your computer and measures how much time you spend on various activities. Then, you categorize those activities from "Very productive" to "Very unproductive." It will then send you out a report and summary every week, helping you understand where your time is going.

Maybe this will drive you crazy, but if you are an analytical person as I am, the app will help you a lot to set some goals around productivity, which is a really cool feature of RescueTime. Each week, I can see if I improved or declined in productivity, and that is a really fun way to challenge myself. I can also view where my time is being wasted which helps me "zap" the unnecessary time spent on foolish tasks.

RescueTime Premium will even help you by blocking distracting websites or sending you alerts if you spend too much time in internet procrastination land. I strongly recommend checking it out.

In fact, a lot of the tips I am going to teach you in the next few chapters come from analyzing my own RescueTime logs over the last few years and identifying what is wasting time. Download the app and try it out. I think you will be surprised to learn just exactly where your time is going every day!

For Further Research:

RescueTime

http://jle.vi/rescuetime

A graphical representation on RescueTime

http://jle.vi/recuetime1

CHAPTER 18: AUTOMATING MEETING SCHEDULING

In honor of Vilfredo Pareto, we'll start with some of the lowest hanging fruit. Let's face it... there are some things computers can do better than humans can. On that note, it turns out one of the biggest ways we waste our time is with scheduling. We have all experienced the situation in which 10 people need to meet, and scheduling the meeting requires 20 emails with the "Reply All" fiasco as everyone lists their available times. Heck, even scheduling one-on-one meetings is a time waster - even if the process is only 2 or 3 emails back and forth.

Instead, you can automate this process by using Doodle. Doodle is an app originally designed for polling people on their availability and notifying all the involved parties when a mutually convenient time has been selected by everyone. Polling is a really great feature, and you should check it out, but actually Doodle is not the tool I use the most. I use their other feature, called MeetMe, for just about every meeting. I know it is impersonal, but I actually sync my entire calendar (without event titles) on the MeetMe page, so people who want to have a meeting can pick times which are convenient for them. I even put in the hours I am sleeping, in case someone from another time zone wants to schedule a call! Once they select a couple times, I log on, pick the time within 10 seconds, and MeetMe adds meeting time to both of our calendars. Amazing!

While I usually have to include a sentence like, "Sorry, I know it is impersonal, but maybe it is easier if you just pick a time on my calendar," I have found people actually really appreciate the convenience. Even close friends book time on my MeetMe page, and I use a customized short link to refer people to the page.

Again, this tip is not for everyone, of course, and there are now a dozen or so competitors out there, but the Doodle Polls are definitely among the most useful I've found, and if you are okay with looking a little snobby, you can save hours every week by never having to send emails like, "Sorry, 8AM does not work for me, how about 9am." What a waste of time!

For Further Research:

Doodle:

http://jle.vi/doodle

CHAPTER 19: TEXT EXPANSION: STOP TYPING THE SAME THINGS OVER AND OVER

As I mentioned in the last chapter, I often repeat the apology warning stating I know my MeetMe page is pretty impersonal. You would be surprised how many times a day you type the same thing, even if it is your username for a website, your phone number, your email, and so on. Typing the same thing over and over can be a huge waste of time, and so I have become a big advocate of a cool method for preventing retyping called "text expansion."

The basic idea is to set up pre-determined shortcuts that "expand" when you type them. Personally, I use a Mac and iCloud, which is great because it syncs all my shortcuts between my iPhone, iPad, and Mac. This is especially useful if you do not want to type things on the small touch screen of a phone. However, there are some great alternatives out there for PC, Android, and so on. I have given a few links to various reviews of the different solutions in the supplemental materials, and I trust you will be able to pick which one suits your needs the best.

If I type the simple phrase "eml", my devices auto-correct to putting in my email address, which is used for most of my logins on websites. This is super helpful if I am on my mobile, where typing an email means switching to symbols to find the @ symbol, and so on.

If I type in "ftpplz," my computer auto corrects "ftpplz" to a long message asking a customer of my software company for their FTP login information and admin credentials, so my technician can do an installation or fix a bug.

I have two different "MeetMe" related ones, ddlcas and ddlpro, which each spit out different sentences encouraging people to book a meeting with me online.

I even have shortcuts for my various phone numbers and addresses (I have a few for the different countries I frequent), sales copy, and more. From time to time, I update, add, or improve these shortcuts, but for the most part, they work great and save me countless minutes every day.

Pretty cool, right? Check out the supplementary materials and download some third-party text expander applications, or, if you are using your an Apple product, navigate to Settings -> General -> Keyboard-> Shortcuts.

By the way, if you're enrolled in the MasterClass, log in now to find a downloadable spreadsheet with all of my recommended expansion shortcuts. You can customize them and copy/paste them into your own devices and save hours of typing and strategizing.

For Further Research:

Android/iPhone Tip: How to create custom keyboard
   shortcuts

http://jle.vi/text1

How to use text expansion to save yourself hours of typing every day

http://jle.vi/text2

Autokey does customized text replacement for Linux

http://jle.vi/text3

Lifehacker Code Texter for Windows

http://jle.vi/text4

CHAPTER 20: SPEAKING IS FASTER THAN TYPING (OR CLICKING)

From the title of this chapter, you probably think I am going to encourage you to use phone calls instead of text messages, or the cool voice-recording feature of iMessage or WhatsApp instead of typing. Well, those are indeed good ways to shave off a few minutes here and there, and you should definitely use them, but you probably already do - so that's not what this chapter is going to recommend.

I am actually just going to recommend you do not type at all.

Okay, that is an exaggeration, but you can actually cut out a lot of the typing you do every day. Let me explain how.

I remember, about 15 years ago, my father got all excited about a software called Dragon Naturally Speaking. "We aren't going to have to type ever again," he said, excitedly opening the box (yes - software came in boxes back then!). Well, in reality, the technology was not nearly there, and my father, like many customers of that type of software, was hugely disappointed. Not much changed up until the last few years, with the developments of a company called Nuance communications and a few others.

As it turns out, most people can comfortably speak at least 120 words per minute, depending on the language, but most can only type around 40 words per minute. Of course, improving your typing speed makes a lot of sense in general, but you will probably NEVER be able to type 120 words per minute, even if you switch to the more efficient Dvorak keyboard.

Fortunately, today, with your iPhone, Mac, Android, or Windows device, you really do not have to type if you do not want to (or if you are not in public). Today, speech-to-text functionality comes built-in to the various mobile and desktop operating systems - and even for older systems, there are third-party apps. I love these features because they save time and reduce issues like carpal tunnel syndrome. In fact, a great majority of this chapter was dictated to my Mac and typed out automatically... which definitely saved me a lot of time.

Let me give you an idea of how this works. On your iPhone you have a key on the keyboard in many languages that will automatically start transcribing spoken text. You would be totally amazed at how fast you can speak (even if you have an accent), and it will still catch what you are saying!

On the Mac, you can set up speech dictation on more recent versions of the operating system, such as Yosemite or Mavericks. You can also set up keyboard shortcuts to make it convenient to use. If there are mistakes, they will usually be underlined in blue as areas of uncertainty, which you can right click, and there will usually be the correct phrase there for you to select.

By the way, this works with a lot of other languages, too. Я тоже могу говорить по-Русский (I can also speak in Russian), which is great, because typing in Russian is often really slow for me. In fact, I also find speaking numbers, like "Call 0522452342" or filling in credit card details is much faster if you do not have to look at the numbers and then type them. I will often read off my credit card or passport number into the computer to avoid having to type the numbers.

This is cool because it allows you to do other things with your hands while typing out emails or even essays. Of course, as I mentioned, not all multitasking is good multitasking, but if dictating emails helps pass the time faster while doing a hard workout, or if exercising while writing your next book gets the creative juices flowing, that is a great use of technology to empower the GOOD kind of multitasking.

My recommendation here would be to get a pair of headphones with a microphone to take advantage of this tip. To avoid embarrassment, it might be better if your friends and colleagues think you are on the phone, rather than if they think you are talking to Hal or Nightrider. If you can get over a little bit of social embarrassment or just pretend you are talking on the phone, you can save a ton of time by minimizing your daily typing.

On another note, I also find I save a lot of time by using voice commands, not just voice to text. Whereas Android has the "OK Google" feature and Windows 8 has Speech Recognition, iOS devices have Siri. Voice commands may not seem like a big time saver, but I find that by bypassing the process of unlocking my phone, finding the right app, clicking the right menus, typing, and hitting save, I can save 2-3 minutes of time and hassle. This applies to all kinds of things I do, including telling Siri to draft my emails, add things to my calendar or to-do list, and looking things up for me.

So, check out the built-in or third party speech to Text features available on your various devices and see how you can save time and reduce muscle fatigue.

For Further Research:

Windows Speech Recognition

<u>http://jle.vi/speech1</u>

Apple Speech to Text Tutorial

<u>http://jle.vi/speech2</u>

CHAPTER 21: USING GESTURES TO SPEED UP COMMON TASKS

Now we have started to shy away from a lot of the manual clicking around and typing which has been wasting countless minutes in our day and distracting us from actually creating productive work, let's take things a bit further.

Did you know you can set automated shortcuts or gestures on your computer to speed up things you frequently do? This goes way beyond the standard keyboard shortcuts you probably already use every day such as Open, Save, Copy, Paste, and so on. Instead, using gestures can dramatically change the way you use apps and the different things you do.

On the mac, we have a really great big trackpad, and a special app I love called BetterTouchTool or BTT. This tool allows you to create ANY kind of gesture - one finger, two finger, three fingers, four... and different patterns of movement. Then, you can assign just about any keyboard shortcut in the computer to a gesture, which saves you from having to memorize all the keyboard shortcuts.

You can also use BetterTouchTool to automatically snap to different sizes of windows, move windows across monitors, and lots of cool features. It even works with Apple Remotes, Magic Mouses, and the Leap Motion touchless controller. In the next chapter, we are going to learn how to string together multiple actions - like opening up a few programs you use together - all with one hotkey. That will make BTT even MORE useful, because you can string things together. One of the coolest BTT shortcuts I have is I can click 5 fingers on my trackpad, and my computer will open my favorite movie-watching app, turn on Airplay, move the app to my big screen TV, and then dim and change the colors of all the smart lights in my house, turning off the ones which aren't in my living room. I am sure you are curious how that works, but we will get to that in a couple chapters from now.

For now, let me share with you some of my favorite uses for BTT, which save me lots of time and keep me from having to use the mouse. I am also including a blog post I wrote a while back sharing all of my configuration specs so you can duplicate them. (If you're enrolled in the MasterClass, head over to the course to download the importable preference files, too!)

-Three finger gestures to forward, reply, or archive mail (depending on the direction)

-Rotating fingers left or right to switch tabs in my browser or chat window

-Four finger taps to maximize windows

-Five finger taps to move windows to my other screens

-Three finger "click swipes" with different option key variations to make windows quarter size, half size, or third size of the page

...and much, much more.

This may not sound like it saves a lot of time, but it goes beyond shaving off the 10 seconds here and there to select things or drag windows. It keeps me from getting distracted or frustrated when I have to mouse to the other end of the screen to perform simple actions. It is something small, but I think it will help streamline a lot of your work. These shortcuts are one of the reasons I can often go through 50 emails in 10 minutes!

In the next chapter, we are going to take it even further than gestures or minimizing typing - we are going to learn how to "act without doing."

For Further Research:

BetterTouchTool

http://jle.vi/bettertouchtool

Turn any action into a keyboard shortcut

http://jle.vi/gestures1

Using Custom Gestures for Improved Work Efficiency

http://jle.vi/gesture2

CHAPTER 22: LAUNCHERS: ACT WITHOUT DOING

One of the biggest areas where we can minimize time wasting and create efficiency is in all the time we spend every day mousing around our computer, searching for files, adding people to emails, drafting emails, resizing images, moving files, and just clicking around. Things like minimizing, adding, updating, and checking – all of this stuff takes a ton of time.

Because of this, there is a class of applications called "launchers." I'm going to be demonstrating a tool on the Mac which is called Quicksilver.

This chapter was originally taken from a screencast video lecture, so please excuse the anticlimactic screenshots that will try to capture Quicksilver's raw power.

What Quicksilver promises is that it lets you act without doing. So, really quickly, let me demonstrate what that means, and then I will walk through essentially how we set it up, and things we can do with it, and so on.

Say I have a customer who calls me on the phone and says "I didn't get the user's manual." Well, really easily, I find the user's manual.

No, it's actually not this one. He needs the deluxe version.

I email it to him. .

Hit tab to move from block to block
Quicksilver uses an "Item > Action > Destination" format

And then I ask him what his email is. Now if he is someone in my contacts I can just say great.

Then hit enter and it is sent.

...then hit Enter
The action you've specified is performed in the background!

And that's it. The email is done. It's actually sent. No problem. In fact, if he wasn't in my contacts, that is also not a problem. Because I can just select "Email to..." and then type his email in the third block, and it is sent. I even have already preconfigured a message that says, "Hey here is the document you requested."

Hit "."at any time
To enter plain text like emails, URLs, or messages

So... pretty cool. But actually, you can do all kinds of different steps with Quicksilver.

For example, say I need a version of a logo scaled to 50 percent.

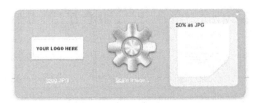

Done, the file is already saved to the directory at 50 percent size. Now I want to access that file without a hassle. You can see that local one right here has been created.

And if I wanted to, I could just hit enter to open it. But actually, I don't want that file there... so I'm going to move it to the desktop.

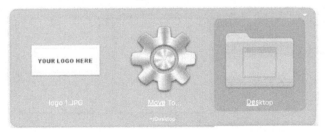

Done.

But it actually gets better.

That's because plugins and preferences extend Quicksilver's functionality to almost anything you can imagine.

So let's look at some of the different stuff that Quicksilver can do for us. If you go into the preferences, you can see that there is a lot different confusing actions.

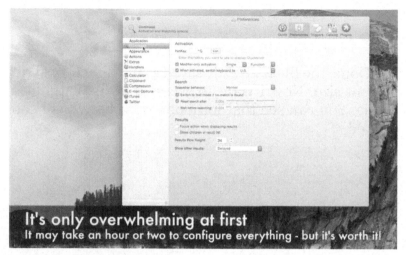

It's only overwhelming at first
It may take an hour or two to configure everything - but it's worth it!

We will look at setting up the different plug-ins. You should look at all of the different kinds of applications that Quicksilver works with.

Set up the different plug-ins. You should really take the time to go through all these plug-ins and see which plug-ins you want to use.

Once you have all of your plug-ins set up, you have preferences for all of the different actions.

Not all of them are going to be useful. Go through all the actions and take the time to figure out how to use the different actions.

There is also something very cool called triggers.

Check out triggers
Triggers let you set keyboard shortcuts for any complex series of actions

I highly recommend taking the time to set up Quicksilver. It can save you a ton of time mousing around, finding different files on your computer, emailing them, uploading, nearly anything that you want to do.

If you are operating on a Windows machine, there is no Quicksilver, but there are some great alternatives you can check out. We have given you a link to a Lifehacker article where you can check out the alternatives and choose the one that is going to be the best for you.

For Further Research:

QuickSilver for Mac

> http://jle.vi/quicksilver

A beginner's guide to Quicksilver

> http://jle.vi/quicksilver2

QuickSilver for Windows Showdown

> http://jle.vi/quicksilver3

LaunchPad for Windows

> http://jle.vi/launchpad

CHAPTER 23: WASTING LESS TIME READING AND SORTING THROUGH EMAIL

At this point, we have learned how to speed up the process of inputting text and sending emails a lot faster. We have also learned how to use keyboard shortcuts to send emails faster.

What about speeding up the process of getting through all of your email? I know this is something that takes a lot of time for most people, and it used to take a lot of time for me until I discovered a service called Unroll.Me.

Unroll.Me is a free service, and basically what they do is connect to your email and intercept certain emails that you have determined may or may not be important. This is not only cool because they can actually help you unsubscribe much more easily, but also sometimes in some scammy emails, the unsubscribe button actually does not work. It just confirms that you received the email enough to click.

But Unroll.Me is much, much more than just unsubscriptions. They also let you create something called a "rollup," and you can read what you want when you want. For your convenience, they have a web-based interface that I'm going to show you really quickly on my email.

Here is an example of a rollup.

I have a rollup for every single day and it is categorized and so you can see here is a trip that someone wants me to go on. Here is a email from the Craig's list equivalent here in Israel. I don't really need to read these.

Another thing that is really cool is that I can actually edit my subscriptions.

So when I get emails, for example, these are the different services I allow to send me email. I also have unsubscribed from over 300 different services that I don't find interesting.

When you first sign up for Unroll.Me, they will scan through all of your email, and they will tell you here is what is interesting or not interesting and you can pare down your email dramatically right from the get-go.

In my Rollup, I have almost 500 different emails that get intercepted, and in addition to the web interface and the iPhone app, those emails come in as a daily "rollup" email. Let me show you what that looks like really quickly.

There's a daily email that comes into my normal email client. This is Mail.app on my Mac, but it will also come into your Outlook, or your Gmail, or whatever it is you want to use.

I don't actually have to open these emails and delete them; I just quickly scroll through every day. I don't need to open up any of these emails unless they are interesting. If I *do* want to open them up, no problem. I just click and it will take me to that email on the web site.

If I want to look at it in my mail client, that's also no problem.

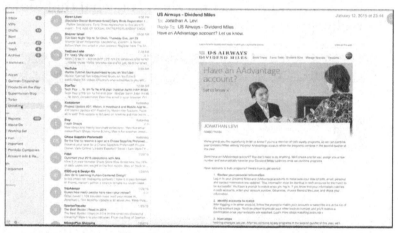

In my IMAP folders, I have a handy Unroll.ME folder where they basically put all of these rolled-up emails. If I want to look at the email in its original context, that is no problem. I can check it out. All the links are there, too. The email hasn't been deleted or modified in any way - just taken out of my inbox and out of my sight unless I want to see it.

Unroll.Me is a really great service. It is completely free. They make it super easy for you to unsubscribe or rollup your emails, and for this reason, I strongly recommend checking it out. It saves me at least 30 minutes a day of deleting spammy emails and junk I don't want to look at.

For Further Research:

Unroll.me

http://jle.vi/unrollme

CHAPTER 24: AUTOMATING SIMPLE REPETITIVE TASKS EFFECTIVELY ACROSS THE WEB

So, in the last chapter I promised to explain to you what IFTTT is, and I think now we are ready.

We know how to use keyboard shortcuts and gestures, we know how to act without doing - but now, it is time to learn how to make the Internet work for us.

IFTTT (If This Then That) is a service that lets us link together different apps across the web to automatically perform actions based on different triggers.

That's a bit confusing, so let me explain by offering some recipes I have personally developed or borrowed from others to speed up things which were taking as much as 10 or 20 minutes EACH - and now take absolutely 0 time.

1) Automatically emailing me when one of my favorite TV shows comes out, so I don't have to keep track of holiday schedules, search TV guide, or miss episodes.

2) Updating all my social media profile pictures - when one changes, they all change.

3) All the accounting for my software side business is done automatically via IFTTT. When we get a sale, the financial details are scraped from the email receipts and input into our Google Drive spreadsheet, in the exact right format for our accounting.

I also recommend using IFTTT to keep you updated with summaries of the news and weather, to control your lights or thermostat, to record different things like check-ins at the gym, and much more. Like

Quicksilver, IFTTT is limited only to your ability to get creative and learn how to make the most of it. You can easily save 2-3 hours a week spent on completely ridiculous tasks like adding lines to spreadsheets and checking the weather report, but of course, you have to invest some time in the beginning.

For Further Research:

IFTTT:

http://jle.vi/ifttt

CHAPTER 25: WATCHING LECTURES, VIDEOS, AND PODCASTS FASTER

If you spend time watching lectures, you know they require a big time commitment, especially if the lecturer is speaking at a slow pace. This is a particular problem for students of my SuperLearner course, who become accustomed to consuming information very rapidly. For them, it is somewhat torturous to sit and listen to someone lecture at 120 or 130 words per minute.

Whether or not you've taken my SuperLearner course and are able to process information at, say, 2-3X speed, you can still shave off a considerable amount of time by just speeding things up to 1.5X, without sacrificing quality or understanding of the material. You have a few options for doing this.

One, you can make sure you're signed up for YouTube's HTML5 player. This is their new technology, which allows 2X speeds, but does not work for YouTube videos past a certain age, does not work for Vimeo, and does not work for a lot of other sites where you may stream flash videos.

In that case, what you should go with is an app called MySpeed which works for Windows and Mac. MySpeed gives you a little slider you can use to speed videos up (or down, but who wants to do that).

MySpeed is a little bit expensive at $30, but allows you to speed up any video, flash, or HTML5, using keyboard shortcuts. You can hit faster, faster, faster, or you can hit your preferred speed. I personally choose to watch videos at 2x speed. This means I can consume lectures faster, but also means I can catch up on my guilty pleasure TV Shows like Big Bang Theory in 11 minutes, but only if I am pressed for time that week.

Another really cool thing you can do is download the Podcasts app from Apple. They allow 1.5x and 2X speeds, and is a great way to consume your news or other information very quickly.

The same is true of the Audible app from Amazon, which lets you listen to audiobooks at a customizable speed.

It might sound a little crazy, but for those of you who are very busy and need to keep up to date on different streaming lectures, podcasts, and so on, speeding up even a little bit can make the process faster and more efficient.

That is enough of the computer productivity hacks. Let's move into some "real life" scenarios where we can shave off wasted time and optimize our performance, shall we?

For Further Research:

YouTube HTML5 Trial

> **http://jle.vi/youtubehtml5**

MySpeed

> **http://jle.vi/myspeed**

Section 4: Speeding Up Health and Fitness

CHAPTER 26: GETTING FIT IN FEWER HOURS

Whenever I ask people what they would do if they had more time, a few of the same things come up. One of the most common ones is "I would get back into the gym and go 3 or 4 times a week." Indeed, physical fitness is extremely important part of our lives, and as I mentioned earlier, physical activity and being in shape can make us more effective in every other aspect of our life by improving our focus and mental acuity.

But who has the time to go to the gym for 2 hours 4 times a week? Well, as it turns out, not only is that unnecessary, it can be detrimental to your health. Overtraining is just as bad as not training at all - and maybe even worse.

Fortunately, a lot of recent research has identified a new type of training which is more effective than the long, two-hour weightlifting and running exercise routines of the 80's. It is called High Intensity Interval Training, or HIIT.

The basis behind HIIT is to do short, intense bursts of exercise, interrupted by short breaks. This applies not only to cardiovascular health, where you should do a series of sprints for a few minutes rather than run 10 miles, but also to weightlifting, where one very intense, heavy set of slowly raising and lowering the weights until muscle failure can have more of an effect on muscle growth than doing 5 sets of 12, for example.

HIIT is a really cool metabolic hack, because it actually conditions the body to speed up metabolism and muscle repair *more* than if you were doing long, exhausting workouts. It also makes your body burn fat like crazy - speaking from experience. The idea is to do the bare minimum to stimulate muscle growth and development, without doing the kinds of damage or micro-tears necessarily associated with exercise. There is a fine line, and if you can hit it, your body will stimulate growth and speed up your metabolism without having to do the repair work. In fact, you do not even need to go to a gym to do HIIT work. You can do HIIT with squats, pull-ups, push-ups, and sprints, which saves you the time of driving to the gym and back!

Remember, I told you that we would use Pareto's Law in all kinds of different ways throughout the course. This is a perfect example. HIIT workouts of 20-30 minutes (including cardio AND weightlifting - seriously!) are the 20% of the work yielding 80% of the results. For this reason, I am a big advocate of CrossFit. A typical workout is 60 minutes, but includes 10 minutes of warmup and 10 minutes of stretching after the workout. The workout itself consists of 25 minutes of strength training, because there is a lot of rest in between sets, and usually a very fast-paced, intense workout of 15 minutes.

Yep, 15 minutes!

It is hugely efficient, and will speed up your metabolism and stimulate growth like you wouldn't believe. This is not only because it is intense and fast-paced, but also because it is stimulating the larger muscle groups like your glutes, quads, hamstrings, and more, which stimulate human growth hormone production and testosterone.

I am going to give you guys some links in the supplementary materials, including a link to Tim Ferriss' blog explaining how he gained 34 pounds of muscle in just 4 weeks, while losing 3 pounds of fat. He did this without illegal drugs, and with about an hour a week at the gym - amazing. Check out HIIT, see which exercises such as kettle bell swings and squats make the largest impact, and you will be amazed how quickly you can work out and see huge performance gains.

For Further Research:

The 4Hour Body – Amazon

http://jle.vi/4hb

The Four Hour Body – iTunes

http://jle.vi/4hb1

From Geek to Freak

http://jle.vi/fit1

High-intensity interval training – Wikipedia

http://jle.vi/fit2

What Is The Best HIIT Workout?

http://jle.vi/fit3

CrossFit – Wikipedia

http://jle.vi/crossfit

Chapter 27: Spend Less Time Cooking

Cooking can take up a lot of time. If it didn't, fast food wouldn't be a $200 billion dollar industry in the US alone.

The truth is, though, that cooking does not have to take nearly as long. By eliminating 20% of tasks which take 80% of the time, or stretching them out across multiple meals, we can actually make things a lot faster.

What exactly do I mean by this?

Well, let's start with chopping and slicing. I was listening to a podcast recently where Andrew Zimmern was a guest, and the host asked him to give one tip to people listening who wanted to make more time for cooking instead of eating out. His tip? Invest in your knife skills. If you are holding the knife and object you are cutting improperly, it will slow you down quite a bit.

The cooking of the food itself is pretty negligible in terms of time commitment, because you can usually walk away and do something else while the water is boiling or the oven is running. In fact, if you ever watch Iron Chef, you see how fast they are able to prepare meticulous meals with no preparation - and a large part is because they spend very little time on chopping.

Most people, however, chop very, very slowly, protecting their fingers. I am going to provide some supplementary videos from YouTube teaching you how to handle a chef's knife correctly, and you will be amazed you can cut at least 50% of your cooking time by using the proper techniques.

The next thing we can do is amortize (or spread out) the preparation and cleaning time. If you are like me, the majority of your "cooking" time is actually "cleaning" and "prep" time - cleaning up the kitchen before you cook, buying all the ingredients, unpackaging them all, boiling water, heating the oven, and of course, scrubbing the pots and pans when you are done. It is hugely wasteful to do this all for just one meal, and so I have learned to cook in bulk. What I will often do is cook enough for 3-4 meals at once - for example, cooking an entire chicken or salmon, and a few pounds of vegetables. Then, I decide if the meal is something I want to eat again tomorrow. Sometimes, the meal is so tasty, I do not mind to eat it 2 days in a row. But other times, I make nice little pre-packaged Tupperware meals and put a few of them in the freezer, where they are good for literally a month.

I know what you are thinking... gross! But actually, if you have a decent freezer, seal the meals in decent Tupperware, and you freeze them right away, the food comes out just as tasty and does not get dry or chewy at all - seriously! If you do not believe me, next time you are at an average restaurant, ask the waitress which items on the menu have been frozen - the answer will surprise you.

Anyways, I do this "bulk and freeze" method at least once a week when I have time and motivation to cook, and at any given time, I will have 2-3 different choices of meals I have cooked over the last couple of weeks. I have amortized my efforts (or batched like tasks) and do not have to shop or clean pots and pans every time I want to eat a nice, home-cooked meal.

Whoa. Did I just shave an hour off of your daily housework *and* an inch off of your waistline? Now *that's* multitasking. Try it out!

For Further Research:

Proper Knife Skills and Technique – YouTube

http://jle.vi/cooking

CHAPTER 28: SLEEPING LESS AND FEELING BETTER

In this chapter, we are going to talk about how you can sleep fewer hours and feel even better.

Wait - what?

I know, I know. All the common sense says you should be sleeping more, not less. Sleep is so hugely important for every aspect of your health - physical fitness and recovery, brain health, focus, and more. But what if I told you that for most people, sleeping 8 hours is actually worse than sleeping 7 and a half? Or that sleeping 7 hours is worse than sleeping 6?

It sounds strange, but it is actually true. You see, for most of us, we have 90-minute sleep cycles where we dip in and out of deep sleep. If you wake up in the middle of a sleep cycle, you will actually feel groggy and exhausted throughout the entire day, even if that means you slept more.

I figured this out when one of the companies I invested in was launching during the same week I was leading an executive board retreat. I only had time to sleep 4 and a half hours each night, but somehow, I felt amazing in the morning. I just needed about a 20-minute nap in the afternoon and I was ready to bounce back.

It turns out I was unknowingly experimenting with something called **polyphasic sleep**. In this case, I was on a *biphasic* sleep schedule, which turns out to be healthier and more natural than monophasic sleep. You see, because of modern electricity and the fact that we work in offices, not out in nature, we have become accustomed to waking up in the morning and staying awake until the evening - but that is really not natural.

In experiments where people are secluded without clocks or distractions, they actually naturally gravitate towards sleeping twice a day. You can probably relate to this, because you probably get really tired every day at around 3 o'clock.

In my other course, I give a lecture just about sleep and napping. I am a huge advocate of napping - and I take a 22-minute nap almost every single day. This nap has allowed me to sleep on average 6 hours a night for the last few years. Your math is correct; my day is about 2 hours longer than yours. Occasionally, I sleep in on the weekends, but for the most part, I have found it to be true that for every sleep cycle I cut out of my nightly sleep, I need one 22-minute nap.

This coincides with a lot of research and experimentation from other polyphasic sleepers, some of whom take it to the extreme and cut all complete sleep cycles, instead taking only six 20-minute naps every day. I definitely do not recommend this approach, but I *do* recommend you start adjusting your sleep to be in multiples of 90 minutes. If your lifestyle affords it, you should try cutting your sleep down by one sleep cycle and squeezing in an afternoon nap.

Even if you cannot cut sleep cycles, you can optimize your sleep in other ways so that you do not need to sleep 8 hours. By the way, the "8 hours" number we have all been told is totally bogus. In tons of military research in dozens of countries, it is been determined everyone has different sleep requirements, and for many of us, 6 hours is a perfectly fine amount of sleep, especially if napping is available. It should be noted, though, on average, women need a little bit more sleep than men need for biological reasons that we will not get into.

You should optimize your sleep by following these important rules:

-Make sure your room is as dark as possible, with no LED's or light coming in from the street

-Avoid blue light at night - buy adjustable smart LED light bulbs if you can afford them or yellow-colored light bulbs if you cannot, install f.lux on your computer, and avoid using your phone in bed. Blue light tells the brain it is daytime and keeps you awake

-Sleep in a cold room with a warm blanket - you can go as low as 64 Fahrenheit or 18 degrees Celsius, though that might be a bit cold for you

-Go to sleep and wake up at the same time every day

-Have a snack immediately before bed. Depending on if your goal is to lose weight or gain muscle, this snack should vary, but it is not a bad idea to have a natural fat source like peanut or almond butter before bed. This will keep your body nourished and prevent the "exhausted" feeling in the morning

-Take magnesium before bed to help your body sleep

-Never use a snooze alarm! Instead, use an adaptive alarm like Sleep Cycle which measures where you are in your sleep Cycle, and wakes you up at the optimal time to prevent grogginess

-If you can afford those smart LED bulbs or some other kind of smart lighting system, use light to wake you up. Getting light into your eyes releases the hormones which wake you up and make you alert - so this also means try to avoid using sunglasses first thing in the morning

Anyways, I am going to link you to some podcast episodes I have done with the world's top sleep experts. I will also link you to the apps I mentioned above, as well as some great articles about polyphasic sleep and light. Check them out and see how you can optimize your sleep to be more effective and efficient.

For Further Research:

Polyphasic sleep – Wikipedia

http://jle.vi/sleep1

Beginners Start Here | Polyphasic Society

http://jle.vi/sleep2

Sleep Cycle for iPhone

http://jle.vi/sleepcycle1

Sleep Cycle for Android

http://jle.vi/sleepcycle2

Sleep Hacking Course on Udemy

http://jle.vi/sleephacking

11 Tricks for Perfect Sleep – Huffington Post

http://jle.vi/sleep3

Philips Hue Wireless Lighting, Starter Pack 110V (US/CA) – Amazon

http://jle.vi/philipshue1

Philips Hue Wireless Lighting, Starter Pack 220240V – Amazon

http://jle.vi/philipshue2

Jonathan's Podcast Interview with Sleep Coach Nick Littlehales

http://jle vi/sleep-coach

Jonathan's Podcast Interview with Sleep Expert Dr. Kirk Parsley

http://jle vi/kirk-parsley

Section 5: Automating Your Finances

Chapter 29: Monitoring Your Finances Automatically

Now that we have covered most of the quick wins we can make in our lives with cooking, sleeping, and fitness, let's talk about another big aspect of everyone's life: finances.

Financial responsibility is important, of course; we need to make sure we are not being charged for things we didn't order, ensure we are meeting our financial goals, and make sure we do not miss payments or incur interest on things like our mortgage, rent, or credit card. All of this does not mean it has to take up a lot of your time.

I remember when I was a kid, my mother would sit for hours every month, going through the credit card statements, tracking expenses, and making sure there were no suspicious charges. Not to mention tax time, when the entire family would sit and sort through receipts and expenses. Most people I know spend an hour or two every month going through their bank statement and credit card statements at the very least, or recording and tracking budgets manually in some extreme cases.

Remember how I told you earlier on in this course there are some things a computer can do better than you can?

This is definitely one of them.

Instead of going through your credit card line by line and making sure there are no fraudulent or unwanted charges, you can take advantage of very sophisticated and powerful software algorithms, such as those offered for FREE by a company called BillGuard. What BillGuard does is connect securely and safely to all of your credit card accounts, and then warn you when they see suspicious or unwanted charges. A lot of these charges are "Grey" charges, which aren't necessarily fraud, but are little things which show up on your credit card that you probably do not want, such as renewal fees for pesky online services you tested out, or hidden changes in prices from your cable provider. The best part is, they automatically alert you of these charges, and give you a fast and easy way to report the charge and get your money back, saving you tons of time hunting for the right phone number or waiting on hold with different credit card companies or service providers.

To date, they have helped people get back over $60 million! This fraud protection allows you to skip reading your credit card statement line by line, and saves you hours each month.

BillGuard also has some great tools for tracking your expenses, but for tracking expenses, I am going to recommend a couple other services which automate budgeting and expense tracking. The first is called Mint.com, which is a company bought by financial software industry leader Intuit. Mint hooks up to all of your bank accounts, credit cards, and other accounts, and tracks all of your spending. It also lets you make awesome budgets, tag and categorize expenses, and easily search all of your financial activity in one search.

Mint then will send you alerts when there are unusually large charges, or when you exceed your budget in a specific category. This can save you time in two ways.

The first is that it helps you automatically budget and track expenses effortlessly, saving you from counting up receipts if you are the type of person who likes to know what you are spending on what.

The second way is that when it comes time to do your taxes, you can save many, many hours of searching through receipts and invoices. Personally, I just create a tag for all tax-deductible business expenses and write-offs, and at the end of the year I am able to quickly total them up from Mint.

Another automatic monitoring solution I want to propose is a new one, and it is actually run by former Intuit CEO Bill Harris. It's called Personal Capital. They offer a free service similar to Mint.com's. The difference with Personal Capital is it offers much more in-depth and sophisticated tracking of investment portfolios, which can save you a lot of time spent (or, in most cases time which should be spent but is not) reviewing your investments and ensuring things are in tip-top shape. For a fee, Personal Capital will also use software algorithms to create and rebalance an optimal stock portfolio for you, saving you the dozens of hours of researching stocks and balancing your portfolio that you probably do not have the time, patience, or energy to do now.

But what about keeping tabs on your credit score, and making sure people are not applying for loans in your name? For that, you should check out a great site called CreditKarma. This site automatically scans your credit score and will alert you if something fishy is happening while you sleep. It does a great job estimating what your credit score is, which means you do not need to do the annual "credit check" from the 3 bureaus, which is a huge time waster. Best of all, it is completely free.

All of these apps have desktop, web, and tablet versions, which makes checking your finances a great candidate for "filler" time we talked about earlier. You can get a quick and complete overview of your entire financial life in a matter of minutes with these apps, which frees you from manually laboring through, monitoring, and calculating expenses.

Check them out and see how much time you can save.

For Further Research:

BillGuard

http://jle.vi/billguard

Mint

http://jle.vi/mint

Personal Capital

http://jle.vi/personalcapital

Credit Karma

http://jle.vi/creditkarma

CHAPTER 30: PAYING BILLS AUTOMATICALLY

The next place we can shave a lot of time is with check writing and paying bills. Since we have BillGuard and Mint.com watching our back, there is not a need or a reason to review our bills before paying them. Now, if you are like me, you may have started paying your bills all online years and years ago. But I still know a number of people who spend an hour or more every single month writing checks, addressing envelopes, adding postage, and mailing them out.

What a waste of time!

Maybe you automatically pay some of your bills, but not others. Maybe you already pay your bills online, but you are guilty of logging on every month to do the payments one by one.

This is yet another area where computers are more effective than humans are. Computers do not forget dates, send payments in late, or transpose numbers. Computers know the exact amount and do not have to look up the bill online. For this reason, I want to encourage you to pay as many bills as possible automatically. In fact, I would argue unless you have some kind of weird payment, almost every monthly bill or payment can be done automatically - even checks to individuals can be automatically sent by your bank, usually at no charge, or, of course, you can set up automatic wire transfers.

Another great benefit here is if you pay bills with credit cards, you have added protection if you are unhappy with the service, and of course, you earn lots of rewards points, depending on your credit card. I offer an entire other course on how to earn lots of miles and fly for free, but that is beside the point...

Consider that most people have a rent or mortgage check, an internet and cell phone bill, a cable TV bill, electric, gas, water, homeowner's association dues, and at least one credit card bill. Imagine each one takes a conservative 5 minutes to open the paper bill (something I avoid like the plague), check the amount, write a check, add a stamp, and seal an envelope. That is almost an hour of check writing you do each month - and that is with conservative estimates, assuming your checkbook is handy and not buried away in a drawer somewhere. That hour would be better spent with family, friends, or doing that Yoga class you have been meaning to get to.

This is not to mention any checks or payments YOU receive, which take 20 minutes of driving to the bank and back, dealing with the ATM, etc. So, the same principles apply - ask your employer or anyone who writes you a check to auto-deposit it into your bank account, and sign up to get a text message when they do so.

So, take a hard look at the time you are spending writing checks, depositing checks, and paying bills, and consider automating as much as possible.

This is a great segue into our next chapter, where we will explore some other things which may or may not be worth your time.

For Further Research:

Ramit Sethi's 12 Minute Guide to Automating Your Finances

http://jle.vi/payingbills1

The Psychology of Automation: Building a Bulletproof Personal Finance System

http://jle.vi/payingbills2

Homework: Set up your bills to pay automatically.

SECTION 6: DELEGATING COMMUNICATION & SAYING NO

CHAPTER 31: SOME THINGS JUST AREN'T WORTH YOUR TIME

In the last chapter, I proposed that paying your bills manually, whether by check or online, is a big time waster and takes up mental space and time you could better spend elsewhere. In this chapter, I want to propose that this is just one common example of a large array of tasks that simply are not worth your time. Not only do many of these tasks waste time, but they also waste your attention and mental energy - and as we have said before, that attention and time can be even more precious than time itself.

Now, I do not know what your time is worth to you, how much time you actually have, or what activities you enjoy doing. What I do know, however, is that for each and every one of us, there are some tasks we either hate doing, are terrible at doing, or that simply are not a good use of our time. Let me give you an idea of what I mean.

I am really pretty lousy at cleaning. It takes me a long time, I do an awful job, and I suffer throughout the whole process. Years ago, though, when I first moved out and into my own place, I didn't want to be one of those prissy, spoiled college kids who hires someone to come and clean my dorm room - I mean, how ridiculous would that be, right?

We used to tell a story about one of our fraternity advisors, who was notorious at his university for having a cleaning lady and laundry service tend to all of his cleaning necessities. We all laughed and made fun of him, but in reality, the joke was on us. That advisor knew something we did not yet realize; time is a precious commodity, especially in college, and the 2 or 3 hours a week spent cleaning, washing and folding laundry, and so on, was just not worth saving the money. He knew he was spending so much money on his college education, and should do everything in his power not to skip reading assignments or homework. He also knew he only had a limited amount of time with classmates and people who would become some of his closest friends.

Obviously, this is not for everyone. I know some people who find cleaning therapeutic, and it helps them unwind after a long week. If that is the case, by all means, clean your own place. But if it is not, then why suffer *and* waste time?

Now, maybe it sounds ridiculous to suggest you hire someone else to do things like your cleaning, gardening, and so on - but you probably do this every single day, by going out to lunch during the work week instead of cooking your own lunch in the middle of the work day. There is not really a difference, if you think about it. To further illustrate the point, "outsourcing" some tasks makes a lot of sense.

Let's do a little math problem here with an imaginary currency, since I do not want to offend anyone by making salary assumptions.

Imagine you earn, say, 20 Coffee Beans per hour at your job. It is not a prestigious or particularly high-paying job, but that is a fair rate. Then, imagine you can get your apartment cleaned in 2 hours, at a rate of 15 coffee beans per hour. Also, imagine that because you are not as effective at cleaning as someone who cleans for a living, it will take you at least 3 hours to do as good a job. In reality, if we look at a concept in economics called "*opportunity cost*," and value your time at 20 coffee beans per hour, cleaning your apartment yourself costs you 60 coffee beans, whereas you could get it cleaned for only 30. In fact, even if you could clean as fast as a professional and do the job in just 2 hours, you would still make a "profit" of 10 coffee beans per hour by NOT cleaning your apartment. Of course, I realize that you do not work every waking hour, and so the opportunity cost, or the price of cleaning instead of working, is just an imaginary one. However, I would ask you a simple question; how much is spending time with friends or family, getting to the gym an extra time per week, or just having an extra 2 hours to relax really worth? Is the time not worth spending the 30 coffee beans?

Here is another, real-life example. I have a friend who is a very successful architect and runs his own firm. He was working on a very exciting project in downtown San Francisco and wanted to alert the media to gain some coverage and recognition for his firm. He came to our CEOs' group with a problem; he and his employees were spending lots of time reaching out to media outlets, and they were not having a lot of success. Not only that, but the hours they were spending on chasing down reporters and trying to pitch the story was causing delays in their work pipeline, and preventing him from completing the project on time.

I will never forget what one of the executives said to him. "You know, when I needed to redesign my office, I didn't waste my time - I came to you and you did the redesign in record time. But yet when you need to get press coverage, you waste your time with it. You have to realize there are people out there who are as skilled and efficient at generating PR as you were at redesigning my office - why wouldn't you take advantage of that just to save a few bucks?" In the end, he hired a PR firm for a few thousand dollars, and the project got amazing coverage, without having to delay a multimillion-dollar deal or distract his very highly paid employees.

Now that I have explained, let me give you an idea of things I currently *refuse* to do.

As I mentioned, I refuse in principal to clean my own apartment.

I know. That sounds really prissy and conceited, but it is true. Cleaning is just a poor use of my time, and so besides the occasional wipe-down, I hire a professional to clean my place every other week. The cost is pretty negligible, really.

The next thing is a more recent one. I have decided washing, drying, folding and ironing laundry is not a good use of my time. I am just way too slow, and I do not do a good job, either. Instead, I have found a service to pick up my laundry in bags within 20 minutes, and brings back clean, pressed and folded clothes within 24 hours. I do this every 10 days or so, and the cost is about $20. Seriously - $20. If you imagine it would take me about 2 hours to do all the sorting, ironing, folding, and hanging, this works out to be a cost of $10 per hour saved. Instead, I can invest that time into fun activities, which to me is worth the $10 an hour many, many times over.

Some weeks, I enjoy going to the grocery store and squeezing my own avocados. Other weeks, I do not have time or energy, and I save the hour of labor by clicking the one-click "reorder" button on the supermarket website. The cost of delivery is about $6, and as I mentioned above, that is way below what I value my time and peace of mind.

But these are just a few examples. What kind of stuff are *you* currently doing that is a poor use of your time? Maybe it is leaving work to get to the pet shop and buy dog food before they close. Maybe it is building IKEA furniture. Maybe it is mowing your lawn. If you enjoy doing these activities and find them therapeutic or enjoyable, (or your time really is not worth that much, for whatever reason), then by all means, keep doing them and do not feel guilty. But just know that you have an option, and you should not feel bad about making a conscientious decision to say "no" to things that are not a good use of your time or mental energy.

In the next chapter, I am going to give you some websites and services to help you find people who are better than you at doing the things you are lousy at doing, and give you some background on how to use these services.

CHAPTER 32: THOUGHTS AND TIPS ON "OUTSOURCING"

In the last chapter, I advocated for hiring other people to do the things you are not efficient or optimal at. Now, I want to give you some tools and resources I like for outsourcing common tasks. Unlike Tim Ferriss, I am not going to tell you to hire a personal assistant, because that is something I have had a lot of difficulty with, and I have not been able to find someone I can really rely on until very recently. I have found it often hit-or-miss to work with individual service providers for high-level or critical tasks, because learning how to work with outsourced employees or freelancers is an entire science and skill set for an entirely different book. I have, however, found a lot of great services that speed up individual tasks.

The first one is a site called eLance, now owned by UpWork. Whether I need programming, design work, drafting, editing, analysis, testing, or really any other type of work, I can usually find some great, qualified people for very affordable rates to do that work for me. I am actually pretty decent with Photoshop, but instead of trying to save money and design my own banners for courses, I hire people on eLance. With my upcoming blog and podcast project, I will also hire people to edit my posts and audio recording, because editing is just not a great use of my time. It may take time to learn how to work with freelancers in this way, but once you acquire the skill and meet a few people you can trust, it becomes fast and streamlined.

Another great site you may know about is called Fiverr. On Fiverr, you can pay people as little as $5 to do hundreds of different types of tasks, from animations and graphics to voice recordings and editing. If you are working on a brief for your company and need it proofread (a task that is really hard to do for your own writing), is not it worth the $5 to get the proofreading done by someone else? Lately, I use Fiverr more than any other outsourcing website, because it's fast, easy, and helps you find people with very niche specializations rather than broad generalists.

Another site I used to love when I lived in the US was TaskRabbit. TaskRabbit lets you post different things you need done in the "real world" like running to the grocery store, and people will bid on the task. You pay them a small fee and refund the expenses, and it is all guaranteed and insured by TaskRabbit. I will never forget how a friend from my CEO group paid someone on task rabbit $70 to wait in line for 6 hours for the release of the iPhone 4, so he and his team could have the latest devices on launch day for testing. This may be an extreme example, but he was able to get 2 new iPhones before many other competitors, and it cost him only $12 an hour - an easy to justify expense for your business.

There are a lot of other sites like this you can research. They vary in quality and arrangement, from temporary workers through an agency to full-scale employment agencies that help you find full time workers. In case you're wondering, after going through 3 or 4 services that definitely did *not* work, I finally found my wonderful assistant through Virtual Staff Finder, and she and I have been happy together ever since. I also read a great book by the company's CEO,

Chris Ducker, which prepared me to better manage a virtual team - which has greatly improved my results.

Overall, I am an advocate of outsourcing small or specialized tasks like formatting, editing, graphic and web design, and so on. Though outsourcing is not the panacea solution Tim Ferriss makes it out to be, it can become a critical part of your timesaving tool kit, if you invest in learning how to manage it.

For Further Research:

eLance:

http://jle.vi/elance

Fiverr:

http://jle.vi/fiverr

TaskRabbit:

http://jle.vi/taskrabbit

Virtual Staff Finder:

http://jle.vi/taskwunder

Virtual Freedom by Chris Ducker

http://jle vi/virtual-freedom

CHAPTER 33: SPEEDING UP DECISIONS

Yet another area where people waste a lot of time is in making decisions. We have all experienced scrolling through the list of movies for a half hour trying to choose something, and in the end, giving up on watching a movie altogether. But this can be much more than just the 10 minutes you spend staring at the menu at the restaurant; having difficulty making decisions (or what is called "analysis paralysis") can add 20-30% of wasted time to all kinds of everyday activities such as getting dressed, your three daily meals, grocery shopping, going out with friends, and so on. Not to mention the hours, weeks, and months you can deliberate on big decisions, like which car to buy, which person to date, and so on.

This is just the tip of the iceberg. Indeed, according to Barry Schwartz, author of "*The Paradox of Choice*," having too many choices cannot only make the process of choosing miserable, it can also make us really unhappy with our final outcome. What's more, there is a real phenomenon called "decision fatigue," which basically says that all of the small decisions we make every day are like withdrawals from a pool of decision-making capacity we have every day. The more small choices we make, the less effective we will be at making big ones.

Decision fatigue also causes a phenomenon called "ego depletion," which wears down our willpower, making us more likely to do things like eat unhealthy foods, engage in dishonest behavior, or cut corners on important tasks. This is the precise reason why people who have to make a lot of decisions, such as the late Steve Jobs or Barack Obama, have specified outfits they wear depending on the day of the week - or in Steve's case, the same thing every single day. It is also the reason Barack Obama is one of the only presidents in American history to never make a request of the White House kitchen - he has told them to surprise him every day.

Decision fatigue can certainly cost us a lot of time in and of itself, but it also raises an important question: Would you rather spend twice as much time, pick the perfect option, and ultimately be only 60% happy with the outcome, or, would you prefer to spend half as much time, choose the 2nd or third best option, but be 100% happy with your choice? In some sense, ignorance is bliss when it comes to decision making.

There are a few ways to avoid analysis paralysis, time wasting, decision fatigue, and ego depletion.

One of them is to engineer "automatic" decision-making rules based on external conditions. For example, I have 3 simple rules when I sit down to a restaurant.

First, I ask the waitress what the best dish in the house is. If the dish meets my dietary guidelines, I will order that before looking at the menu.

Second, if the waitress is not available, or I do not like the recommended dish, I look for one of two things I particularly like.

If a restaurant has Salat Niçoise, I will automatically order it without checking the rest of the menu. If they do not, I will look for a grilled filet of Salmon and order that.

When I sit down at an Indian restaurant, I almost always order Chicken Tikka Masala and Palak Paneer. If I am at a Chinese restaurant, it is usually just broccoli beef and Orange chicken with Chicken Low Mein.

This might sound crazy to always eat the same thing wherever I go, but it saves a lot of hassle and in reality these are dishes I really enjoy, so unless I am in a special restaurant known for a special dish, or the waitress or chef has a special recommendation, why waste my energy and risk getting a dish I do not love?

I no longer drink alcohol - a big productivity booster in and of itself. But when I used to order wine, I used a pairing system I have memorized based on what dish I am ordering, and then ask the waitress or sommelier to choose a bottle of specific type of wine for me based on my price range. Let them make the decision and use up their own decision-making points.

These types of rules can apply to all different kinds of conditions. You may not want to become so robotic as to plan an outfit of each day, but what about choosing your shirts in the random order in which they are stacked in your closet, and then having a "matched" pair of pants that go with each one. Effectively, you have chosen a matching outfit without making a single decision. Or how about setting one or two nights a week where you do not have to think about what to cook or eat. Mondays are usually pretty stressful, so why not make every Monday Fajita night?

The next strategy is maybe a little bit morally questionable, but it is basically to offload decisions onto other people. I do not always do this, but if I am having a pretty busy and stressful week where I need my full mental capacity, I definitely am guilty of offloading decisions.

When I travel with friends who do not have my similar "optimization" mentality, I tell them at the beginning of the trip I am happy to go wherever they want to go, eat wherever they want to eat, and do whatever they want to do. I am on vacation - why should I make any choices?

When I go out to dinner with friends, I play the nice, flexible guy and ask them to recommend a favorite restaurant in their area that is convenient for them. When choosing a movie to watch... well, you get the idea.

It is important to note I do not reply with, "I do not know - what do you want to do?" like the scene from the Jungle Book. Instead, I ask for a recommendation and let the other person understand that I want them to be happy with the outcome above all - "Why don't you pick somewhere you like," or "How about you choose a movie you've been meaning to see?"

If other people do not know about the paradox of choice, and the outcomes are more important to them than being happy with the choice, it is a great opportunity for you to skip making a decision, and look like a friendly, easy-going person. Besides, *everyone* loves spending time with people who go with the flow and put other people's preferences first - even if they do not fully understand why!

The last and possibly most important strategy for optimizing decision-making is to limit your choices. It is very easy when you are looking for a solution to research 10 or more solutions, but in fact, you should really limit decisions to 3-5 options, right off the bat. The more possible variables and options you throw in, the more likely you be unhappy, and the more time you will waste. For this reason, you can use different strategies such as *only* looking at the specials menu, *only* scrolling through one page of movies, or *only* purchasing a category of products from one specific brand.

For example, I have decided I only shop at Under Armour for my workout clothes - and even there, there are too many options, so I usually only shop at the "Specials" section of their website. If I were to also shop at Reebok, Nike, Adidas, and Puma, I have added too many extra options, making the process too difficult.

So, while sometimes people at the gym tease me for having Under Armour head to toe, I am saving lots of time and decision fatigue by just purchasing whatever is available at the Under Armour store when I need new gear, and I am always happy with my decisions, because I do not know what kinds of new stuff I am missing out on from Nike. I do not really need to know, either!

By carefully addressing and limiting the amount of decision-making and deliberation we have to do, we save not only time, but also save a lot of mental energy and capacity, which has pretty awesome effects on our performance and efficiency in other aspects of our life.

Give this a try, and check out the TED Talk and book on the Paradox of Choice in the supplementary Materials.

For Further Research:

The Paradox of Choice – Amazon

http://jle.vi/paradoxofchoice1

The Paradox of Choice – iTunes

http://jle.vi/paradoxofchoice2

Barry Schwartz: The paradox of choice – TED.com

http://jle.vi/paradoxofchoice3

CHAPTER 34: SPEEDING UP COMMUNICATION

In the last chapter, we talked a bit about how other people can play a role in our productivity, specifically when it comes to decision-making. In this chapter, I want to take that idea a bit further, and note how communication and dependency on others can play a big role in our productivity.

As human beings, we are social creatures, and this means for most of us, communication will take up a majority of our time. With that said, there are strategies to make communication more efficient, without hurting feelings.

In the beginning of the course, I talked about sending back and forth emails and waiting for responses to move forward. This is something covered in the "Getting Things Done" productivity system, and is called an "Open Loop." An open loop is something that basically drains resources by looping back and forth, such as sending emails back and forth. An example of this is if an acquaintance invites you to a wedding and you reply with "let me check my calendar and get back to you," when in fact you actually mean "thanks, but no thanks." That open loop has created more work for both of you, as they will have to follow up and you will have to write another email or have another conversation.

Now, I am not going to tell you how to communicate with other people. Communication is something only you can judge, and you always should be yourself. However, I will give you some suggestions as to habits you can implement into your communication style.

The goal of making communication more efficient is to be polite yet firm, and always direct. Say what you mean, and mean what you say. Get directly to a solution rather than being indecisive.

Here are some examples:

If you are picking a restaurant with a friend over text message, and they ask you, "Where do you want to go," you already know to avoid the "I do not know, where do you want to go." Instead of writing back, "How about either Cafe Zed or Taqueria," you write back, "Let's go to Cafe Zed."

You just saved 50% of the time in the interaction... but that is just the beginning.

Another important aspect is to tell it like it is. If you do not want to do something, do not leave an open loop - just politely say no. If you have a problem with something, just tell the other person the problem as politely as you can, right when you observe the issue. It will save you both <u>so</u> much time (and hassle)!

If you learn to be direct in your communications and tell people what you expect, want, or need without fuss, you will be amazed at how much faster things happen, and usually without offending anyone. Examples of this include saying things like "If you could, please respond back with the following three things:" instead of vague language and a list of questions. Short, direct communications are magical when it comes to efficiency, and unless you are in a culture where small talk is mandated for every interaction, most people will appreciate you saving their time as well as your own. Just in case, you can always throw in a "sorry to be so direct, but I am sure you are very busy" to let them know you are not doing it out of rudeness. In my experience, most people will appreciate you being considerate of their time.

Give it a try and see where you can minimize wasted effort and time using more direct communication and less indecisive deliberation.

For Further Research:

Getting Things Done – Amazon

http://jle.vi/gtd1

Getting Things Done – iTunes

http://jle.vi/gtd2

Section 7: Conclusion

Chapter 35: A Bonus: Become a SuperLearner And Learn Things Faster

For most of us, reading and learning takes up a majority of our time, and from my perspective, accounts for a majority of our wasted time. We are all confronted with an ever-growing mountain of new information. There are more and more books put out every year, 24 hours of news from all over the world, new scientific and technological breakthroughs every day. It is overwhelming. For this reason, speed-reading and accelerated learning is both a very hot topic and a very important one.

Unfortunately, the process of learning to become a speed-reader, super learner, and so on is far beyond the scope of this course. I will, however, give an introduction to some of the ideas, and offer you a coupon to get a nice discount off my bestselling MasterClass, Become a SuperLearner. If you have enjoyed this book so far, you are going to LOVE that one.

Basically, the principles involved in learning and memorizing faster are as follows:

1) Retraining your eyes to be more efficient in their movement and absorption of information

2) Completely rewiring the way your brain processes information, using faster comprehension techniques like visualization and visual memory

3) Memory techniques for storing and recalling vast amounts of information quickly and accurately

4) Developing the cognitive infrastructure to support this flood of new information long-term

I wish I could give a short explanation on SuperLearning and speed-reading and teach you the skills necessary, because those skills save me *at least* one hour every single day. However, I hope the coupon code is some consolation, and you will invest the time in developing this skill set to further enhance all of your other productivity gains.

For Further Research:

http://jle.vi/bonuscourse

CHAPTER 36: WHAT WE'VE LEARNED AND CONCLUSION

And so, this brings us to the end of the book. Let's have a look back on all the different theories, techniques, and tactics we've learned.

We started out with some background exploration into why we would want to do things quicker, where most people spend time, and understanding how the course was engineered. We also wrote out some goals and areas we want to improve on.

Now is a good time to look back on those goals and priorities and see if we have covered them. Have you learned some strategies that can help you speed up the time-consuming areas you outlined at the beginning of the course?

From there, we dove into foundations and theory, and learned about the power of preparation, and the importance of goals, priorities, and deadlines. We also learned some effective theories such as the Pareto Principal, Parkinson's Law, and batching similar tasks. We talked about the differences between "Good" multitasking and "Bad" multitasking, and discussed the importance of planning in rest breaks for efficiency.

We even covered some strategies for taking advantage of wasted chunks of time, and dove into an abridged discussion on Flow and focus.

From there, we explored some concrete tips and tricks for speeding things up. We heard about speed-reading and memory hacks, a ton of computer productivity hacks, fitness and health optimization tweaks, financial automation tips, and a bit on avoiding unnecessary or inefficient uses of our time.

My hope for you is this course has turned you on to the mentality of a Speed Demon. It may take time for these learnings to settle in and for you to perfect these skills and habits, but I hope they will cause you to look at your productive life a bit differently, and to identify areas where you could leverage your time more effectively or responsibly. I want to make it clear that not *everything* in life is about efficiency and optimization; in fact, all of the tips, theories, and strategies in this book are designed to help you make time for the things that *should not* be optimized; time spent doing things you love with people you care about!

I hope the book has been very helpful, and of course, very productive for you, and I want to thank you for learning with me. I hope you will take some time to leave a review, tell your friends, and share your feedback.

Let me congratulate you on becoming a SpeedDemon!

For Further Research:

Homework: Please write a review of this book! Thank you.

ABOUT THE AUTHOR

Jonathan A. Levi SuperLearner (800+wpm), Life Hacker, Entrepreneur, Investor

Jonathan Levi is an experienced entrepreneur, angel investor, and lifehacker from Silicon Valley.

After successfully selling his Inc 5,000 rated startup in April of 2011, Levi packed up for Israel to gain experience in the Venture Capital industry. While in Israel, Levi enlisted the help of speed-reading expert and university professor Anna Goldentouch and machine learning expert Dr. Lev Goldentouch, who tutored him in speed-reading, advanced memorization, and more. Levi saw incredible results while earning his MBA from INSEAD, and was overwhelmed with the amount of interest his classmates expressed in acquiring the same skill set. Since acquiring this "SuperLearning" skill, he has become a proficient lifehacker, optimizing and "hacking" such processes as travel, sleep, language learning, and fitness. He later collaborated with his tutors, creating the blockbuster *Udemy* course *Become a SuperLearner* among others. More recently, he has founded the *Becoming SuperHuman Blog & Podcast*, a spinoff brand of his successful online courses, and the popular SuperLearner Academy online learning portal.

Levi has been featured in such publications and programs as the *Wall Street Journal, The Silicon Valley Business Journal, Mixergy, TEDx, EOFire, LifeHacker UK*, and Donna Fenn's latest book, *Upstarts! How GenY Entrepreneurs are Rocking the World of Business* and *8 Ways You Can Profit from Their Success*, among other blogs, podcasts, and publications.

SAVE ON OTHER BOOKS AND COURSES

Become a SuperLearner - The Book
http://jle. vi/abook

Become a SuperLearner - The MasterClass
http://becomeasuperlearner.com

Become a Speed Demon - The MasterClass
http://becomeaspeeddemon.com

Interested in all of the above? Check out:
The Learning & Productivity Bundle
http://jle.vi/bundle

Made in the USA
Columbia, SC
03 February 2020